THE SOUND OF
WORLDS COLLIDING

Stories of radical discipleship
from Servants to Asia's Urban Poor

EDITED BY KRISTIN JACK

PO Box 538, Phnom Penh, Cambodia.
PO Box # 88195, Chinatown, Vancouver, B.C. V6A 4A5, Canada.
30 Osborne Road, Earlsdon, Coventry
CV5 6DY, United Kingdom.
Hegenheimerstrasse 193, CH-4055, Basel, Switzerland.
PO Box 259, Red Hill, QLD 4059, Australia.
PO Box 19-404, Avondale, Auckland 1746, New Zealand.

ISBN 13: 978 - 99950

Printed by Hawaii Printing House
Phnom Penh, Cambodia.
2nd printing.

Cover and text design by Paboom
33 Taylor Road, Mangere Bridge, Manukau 2022,
Auckland, New Zealand

Thank you:
to Susan, Kaleb and Emma,
my fellow adventurers sharing this journey with me;
and to Karen Hollenbeck, Steve Westergren, Ross Allan
and Alistair Craig for all your hard work helping to
whip this manuscript into shape.

CONTENTS

We can admire and worship Jesus without doing what he did. We can applaud what he preached and stood for without caring about the same things. We can adore his cross without taking up ours. I had come to see that the great tragedy of the church is not that rich Christians don't care about the poor but that rich Christians don't know the poor. When the worlds of poverty and wealth collide, the resulting powerful fusion can change the world. But that collision rarely happens... I long for the Calcutta slums to meet the Chicago suburbs, for lepers to meet landowners and for each to see God's image in the other. It's no wonder that the footsteps of Jesus lead from the tax collectors to the lepers... (for) when the rich meet the poor, we will see poverty come to an end.

Shane Claiborne, *The Irresistible Revolution*[1]

PREFACE

All of us live with hopes and dreams about how life could be better. For many that usually means how things could be better *for me*. But there are others, in light of the present day realities of global poverty, marginalization and oppression, who dream that *this world* can and should be a better place. Some see this dream for the world mainly in economic, health or educational terms, while some Christians connect this dream with the Kingdom of God, with Jesus' promise of 'life in all its fullness' coming to fruition in people and in their communities, in relationships and economics, in health and education, in having greater opportunities, and in spiritual as well as social transformation. These Christians find their inspiration in the very ancient biblical story of God's desire for mercy and justice and God's concern for the poor and the oppressed (Micah 6:8, Deuteronomy 10:17-19, Psalm 140:12). But for other Christians, the biblical vision for restoration, healing and peace-making remains *only* a dream.

This book traces the stories of a small band of Christian missioners who have heard the heartbeat of God and are seeking to challenge our contemporary way of life by entering into God's passion for restoration and shalom with their whole lives as they join hands with their national friends and colleagues. In this way, they have become a sign, servant and sacrament of the Reign of God in the slums of the major cities in Asia.

These are the stories of hope and longing, not in the security and safety of Western affluence and comfort, but in the midst of a life of identification and companionship with the poor. Thus these

1

are the stories from the underside of history and in the places of degradation and pain.

One may well expect to find only darkness and difficulty in these stories, but the reader will be caught by surprise. For here the threads and colors of hope, transformation, healing and empowerment are ever present, even in the places which the world has all but forgotten and the people who have been left on the ash heaps of 'our progress'.

Like all good stories, these are richly textured and complex, and they can be read from many perspectives.

For the general reader, these pages provide graphic insights into the conditions, needs and challenges facing millions in the slums of Asia.

For the community worker, this book provides a rich resource, told with humility and self-deprecating humour, regarding a range of strategies used in seeking to identify with, journey alongside of and join hands with slum dwellers, in order to see goodness, wholeness and blessing come into their lives and their communities.

For the general Christian reader, this book shows what can be done against seemingly overwhelming odds, not by large development agencies, but by a small 'Gideon's band,' in bringing about healing and social transformation. As such, these stories serve to bring glory to God and give testimony for the way the Spirit is at work in the places among the poor.

For the missioner, these stories demonstrate a vision for incarnational and integral mission that follows the downward mobility of the Son of God (Philippians 2:5-8). This is a missional vision of identification and partnership spawned out of an *imitatio Christi*. It points to new ways of serving the Kingdom of God in the twenty-first century, one that moves beyond older colonial and triumphalistic models of mission.

Like a gold vein throughout these stories runs an emphasis on a missional spirituality that combines prayerfulness with community building, evangelism with social transformation, the work for justice with the creation of beauty. Here is not the old activism of the evangelical 'empire', but an attempt to discern the signs of God's presence in the world and to work *with* God rather than simply *for* God in the inbreaking of God's love, healing and restoration.

Kristin Jack, a leader in Servants to Asia's Poor, has done us all a great service in drawing together these challenging stories and in contributing much from his own extensive missional experience in Cambodia.

It will soon become evident to the reader that this book is not about heroes. It is about ordinary women and men who have heard God's call to side with the poor in Asia and to work with them in order that God's goodness and justice may come more fully in the unexpected and neglected places of our world. And so we thank the many faithful persons in these pages for being signs of hope and a challenge to us all.

Charles Ringma, *Emeritus Professor of Mission Studies, Regent College, Vancouver, Canada*

Introduction

WHAT IS 'SERVANTS'?

Kristin Jack

Servants Asia Coordinator, Phnom Penh, Cambodia

Kristin Jack and his wife, Susan, a doctor, have been living in Phnom Penh since 1994, along with their children, Kaleb and Emma.

> *The Spirit of the LORD is upon me,*
> *Because He has anointed me*
> *To preach the gospel to the poor;*
> *He has sent Me to heal the brokenhearted,*
> *To proclaim liberty to the captives*
> *And recovery of sight to the blind,*
> *To set at liberty those who are oppressed;*
> *To proclaim the acceptable year of the LORD.*
> *(Luke 4:18-19 NKJ)*

This book contains the stories of a small band of very ordinary men and women who have dared to believe an extraordinary dream: that it is possible to take Jesus at his word, and to take seriously his mission mandate among the poor and hurting.

The Vision

In the late 1970s and early 1980s, God spoke to Viv Grigg, a New Zealander living as a missionary in the sprawling metropolis of Manila.[2] Burdened by the poverty and sense of abandonment he saw all around him in the vast slums and squatter areas of the city, Viv Grigg grew strangely dissatisfied with his role as church planter among middle-class Filipinos.

Searching for the cause of his restlessness he began to ask himself, *where would Jesus be, if he were here in Manila?* He climbed to the top of a one-hundred-foot high mountainous pile of rotting, decaying food and rubbish and looked down at the shacks of ten thousand of Manila's poorest, weeping as he and a pastor friend watched two small children pick through the garbage in search of recyclables.

"God, why don't you do something!" he demanded, anger welling up inside him. In response, he heard the quiet voice of God saying, *"But I have done something. Two thousand years ago, I stepped into poverty and I have dwelt there ever since...'Where I am there shall my servant be also.'"*

Viv began to research the needs of these slum and squatter settlements swelling all over Manila, visiting many of them on a motor bike, searching for where God was already at work. As he did so, his heart was burdened by a second tragedy: although many Catholic brothers and sisters were living in obedience to Christ's call to the poor, almost no Protestant missionaries or Protestant churches were living or worshipping among the slums and shanties of this place that was known as 'Asia's most Christian nation'. Those churches that prided themselves on 'preaching the good news' certainly weren't doing it among the poor. In Manila, as in the great cities sprawling all over the two-thirds world now, the urban poor had become the mission-field's largest unreached people group.[3]

Knowing since he was a child that God had called him to go among these poor, Viv found a small room to rent in the sprawling mega-slum of plywood, cardboard, tin and plastic known as Tatalon. The evening he first climbed the ladder to his shanty during a storm that seemed to unleash all the fury of the gods, he sat in prayer asking God, *"Why am I here?"* In the light of his candle, surrounded by his cardboard boxes of possessions, he watched a large gold and white rat walk along the rough wooden rafters that supported the flimsy tin roof, and his thoughts fell on a rough wooden cross. Viv felt God begin to whisper into the very depths of his being: *"You are here to carry my cross! Preach the cross! Plant the cross! It is an instrument of death. You must die to your self in order to be a servant of these people. In it is the salvation of these people: from drunkenness and despair, from broken families and oppression, from poverty and desolation. In it alone is their hope. Remember, it is a rugged cross. Do not return to a tinsel cross. Take up my cross and follow in my footsteps, for I too chose poverty."*

Under the galvanized roof of that first slum home, Viv read about the life of St Francis Xavier, who converted tens of thousands in India and Japan by going first to wash leper's feet, and as he thought of the three million poor living in the slums all across the city of Manila, Viv cried out to God for bands of men and women like Xavier - for an apostolic order of preaching friars and praying intercessors.

Overpowered by this sense of God's heart for the marginalized of the great cities of Asia, and struggling to cope with the demonic powers he encountered, and his lack of skill, experience and organizational structure in the face of this immense task, Viv returned to New Zealand in 1981. There he began to call for companions from among comfortable middle-class educated Christians to come embrace Christ's discipleship in a deeper way to serve the poor. *"God is calling, looking for men and women who will hear his voice and speak his message to people in these cities. God wants to break us down to be grains of wheat that die to ourselves and give our lives to these poor. He asks us to die to privacy, to our*

roles and achievements. As we die, a new life will emerge. " [4] Again
and again he laid the challenge before New Zealand churches and
New Zealand Christians, living in a land of plenty and staggering
natural beauty, asking *"what does Jesus mean when he says we are
anointed to preach good news to the poor?"* Viv refused to play down
either the depth of the burden God had given him, or what it
would cost us to respond. *"Will I become a grain of wheat? Will I
give myself to die?"*[5]

But God was moving, and people responded up and down
the country. By 1982 a new mission was born that would try to
embrace God's burden for these groaning cities: Servants to Asia's
Urban Poor. By 1983, a team of six had formed to train together
before relocating to the slums of Manila; a few months after that,
a second team of eleven followed them (including an Australian
couple as the movement began to internationalize, now drawing
from all over the world). Over time, teams have formed in Thailand,
India, Cambodia, Indonesia and Myanmar (Burma). The gospel
call to preach and be good news to the poor – Jesus' own mission
mandate (Luke 4:18-21) - was once more being heard. It is a sacred
call that has been lost by the church so many times over the
past 2000 years, and it seems that God must continually raise up
prophetic voices to call his people back to this gospel core. Led by
this Spirit, Viv had set in motion a new missionary movement that
would in turn inspire other missions[6] and slumbering churches -
and even several indigenous movements[7] - to awaken and embrace
God's heart for the poor.

The Call

Since that time, determined to be not simply activists, but
'contemplatives in action', Servants workers have spent time
reflecting on *what kind of mission* Scripture, history and context
demand of them. The Servants movement is defined by five
missiological principles: *Incarnation, Community, Wholism,
Servanthood* and *Simplicity.*

Over time, Servants workers have realized that these five
principles – if taken in isolation and lived to the extreme – can
lead to physical and spiritual exhaustion, and so five more values

have emerged as a counterbalance to the core principles: these are *Grace, Beauty, Celebration, Creativity* and *Rest.*

As you read through the following stories it will become obvious how these five core missiological principles have shaped the impact of Servants in Asia (and increasingly, in the West). We believe these were – and still are – the way of Jesus. Now, as then, Jesus himself calls us to live as he lived: empowered by God's Spirit, to take the *idea* of God's love and make it real in our world – yes, to our neighbors, but also to strangers and even to our enemies. As Christians we are faced with a stark and simple choice: to live in love and truth, or to live out a self-serving lie.[8]

To those original fishermen-disciples two thousand years ago, Jesus said 'follow me, and *I will make you into* fishers of all mankind' (Matthew 4:19). By following Jesus into his mission *we* will be transformed. *We* will *become* someone we have never been before. Jesus will teach us how to embrace men and women, not with nets or hooks, but with cords of love, service and salvation.

It's an idea that will change the world, but only after it has changed us first. It is we who will be transformed as we follow Jesus, and as we let him take us among *'these the least of my brothers and sisters'*(Matthew 25:31-46): the lost, the lonely, the impoverished. Then and only then will this world be able to see the transformational power of the Gospel once more at work in their midst.

WHAT IS SERVANTS?

1. Shane Claiborne, The Irresistible Revolution: Living as an Ordinary Radical (Zondervan: Grand Rapids, 2006), 114.
2. You can read the full story of Viv Grigg's original vision and the birth of Servants in his compelling book, Companion to the Poor (Authentic Media, 2006, rev. ed.).
3. In the middle of the first decade of the twenty-first century, world demographics passed a historical threshold: for the first time in all of human history more people lived in cities than in rural areas. This demographic shift will continue to accelerate, particularly fueled by the burgeoning mega-cities of the developing world.
4. Viv Grigg, quoted in Jenni Craig, Servants Among the Poor (OMF, 1998), 27-28.
5. ibid, 31.
6. Other movements that have been influenced or inspired by Viv's original vision include Servants Among the Poor (now Servant-Partners) in the United States, Kairos in Brazil, InnerChange in the United States and Urban Trek of InterVarsity in the United States. This vision has multiplied into now over two hundred works and helped energise and inspire mission movements to the poor all over the globe. (See Urban Leadership database, 2005.)
7. Such as the Encarnação Alliance of Urban Poor Movement Leaders, which is helping to catalyse these indigenous movements and to innovate training processes so that these courageous men and women embracing the Franciscan call can learn from the stories of each other and from those who have gone before them.
8. Matthew 25:31-46; 1 John 4:7-21; James 2:14-19

One

INCARNATION

Love has to become an action or something
concrete... There must be an
incarnation. Love must be made flesh.

Bono[1]

INTRODUCTION: MOVING INTO THE NEIGHBORHOOD

Kristin Jack

When Christ came into the world he said:
"Sacrifice and offerings you did not desire,
but a body you prepared for me...
I said, 'Here I am...
I have come to do your will, O God.'"

(Hebrews 10:5-7)

O f all the principles embraced by Servants, incarnation is perhaps the least commonly understood, and so I want to begin with a thorough explanation of our theology of incarnational mission.

We believe that as God sent Jesus, so he wants to send us; that his mission is our mission; that his way is our way, and that he will anoint with his Spirit all who seek to follow his footsteps.[2] For more than twenty-five years now, Servants has sought to live out this mandate among the least, lost, hurting, and hungry in both Asia and the West. To this end, we have planted churches, discipled and mentored local leaders, educated youth and pastors, worked with street children, drug users, sex workers, HIV/AIDS patients, AIDS orphans, disabled children, and supported local income generation and microfinance, among an ever-growing list of community development projects and initiatives.

And yet, significant as they are, these vibrant ministries are not the core of what Servants is all about. Instead, the heart of our mission is our commitment to simply *be with* the poor, to relocate into their neighborhoods and patiently build relationships, listening to their burdens and dreams, looking to see where the Spirit of God is already at work and offering our hands to come alongside and tend those seeds of God's Kingdom. Any *ministry* activity that subsequently happens *flows out of relationship* with our neighbors and with the community—not simply because some foreign donor or 'home church' thought it would be a good thing to do.

More and more, the desire grows in me simply to walk around, greet people, enter their homes, sit on their doorsteps, play ball, throw water, and be known as someone who wants to live with them. It is a privilege to have the time and the freedom to practice this simple ministry of presence. Still, it is not as simple as it seems. My own desire to be useful, to do something significant, or to be part of some impressive project is so strong that soon my own time is taken up by meetings, conferences, study groups, and work-shops that prevent me from walking the streets. It is difficult not to have plans... not to feel that you are working directly for social change. But I wonder more and more if the first thing shouldn't be to know people by name, to eat and to drink with them, to listen to their stories, and to tell your own, and to let them know with words, handshakes, and hugs that you do not simply like them, but truly love them.

Henri Nouwen[3]

In this, as in all things, Christ is our model: *'The Word became flesh and moved into the neighborhood'.*[4] As Christians, we believe that Jesus was the physical image or representative of God on earth (Jesus said, "he who has seen me has seen the Father"[5]). At the same time, we believe that Jesus became flesh and blood, and that in the thirty-three years that he dwelt on the earth, he wept, laughed, ate, slept, grieved, and suffered—just as we do. To try and explain this profound mystery, Christians throughout history have used the ancient Latin word, *incarnation*, which literally means, "in flesh". When Jesus was born into our world of pain and joy, parties and death, friendship and war, tears and laughter, beauty and suffering, he really did give up any kind of divinity – in fact he *emptied* himself completely, and became as human as you or I. What is even more staggering than God becoming human is that Jesus went even further and took on the nature of a *servant*, loving us, teaching and modeling life for us, and finally dying for us as a result of human betrayal and injustice.[6]

During his physical life on earth Jesus was completely dependent on the Father and on being filled with the Spirit of God to do the work of loving, healing, feeding, and driving out evil spirits.[7] In the same way, we practice radical relocation, choosing to live with the urban poor, learning from them, building genuine relationships, participating in their lives and struggles, learning their language and their culture, and working out how Jesus' love can best be shown in their context. This radical relocation to be with the poor is what has taken some of us across town to 'the other side of the tracks' and many of us across the globe to live with the poorest of the poor crowded into the shanties and slums of Asia's aching mega-cities. That shift to living incarnationally is not always easy, particularly when the local community behaves in ways you not only dislike, but that make you want to crawl under a rock—as you'll read in Dorothy Mathieson's reflection on her choice to join a local church in Manila.

The Bible tells us that "God is love."[8] This is at once the simplest and most profound definition of God's very nature that you will ever find. But if Jesus hadn't come and lived and suffered among us for those thirty-three years, 'love' would have remained forever just a concept, an idea. A beautiful and poetic idea,[9] to be sure, but still just an idea. Love is nothing but a romantic, starry-eyed sentiment until we take the risk of giving it our hands, our feet, our actions. Only then does it become real and touch us with the potential to change our lives and change our world. This is what God did in and through Jesus, and it did change our lives and our world. And this is what we mean by *incarnation*.

In all of the stories that make up this section on "Incarnation", you will hear from an ordinary group of Christ-followers who have sought to live out their lives by saying, along with the Apostle Paul, *"I want to know Christ, and the power of his resurrection and the fellowship that comes from sharing in his sufferings, becoming like him...in his death...and in his resurrection."*[10]

Becoming Real: Integrating The Head, The Heart And The Hand Of Mission

Craig Greenfield

(Phnom Penh, Cambodia)

Craig Greenfield is the International Coordinator of Servants. Though he wrote this article while living in Phnom Penh, working with children orphaned by HIV/AIDS, he and his wife, Nayhouy, and their two children, Jayden and Micah, have since relocated to Vancouver, Canada, in order to begin a Servants community working with the inner-city poor there.

Our first home in Victory Creek Bridge slum was surrounded on all four sides by other shacks. Our landlord completed the enclosure, living below with his boisterous family of at least ten people. Beside our bed was a wall so thin we could hear our neighbor breathing in his own bed each night and through which we could hear them discussing everything from the daily horoscopes to how much they had spent at the market that morning.

The only way for natural light to enter our home was through the one window or the front door. If we shut the front door we were thrust into darkness, so we left it open most of the time and gave up our privacy just the way Cambodians like it.

Passers-by would look up and make comments to us as we washed dishes or came out of the bathroom wearing just a towel. In return, we often saw more of our neighbors than Western modesty permits. All part of slum living.

Our home had two unique features. The first, was an electricity pylon (minus the live wires - to my mother's relief!) bizarrely built through the middle of our simple concrete bathroom (which contained a squat toilet and a bucket for washing), and towering over our little house like some futuristic steeple. We often used that pylon as a landmark for directing people to our home,

"Just cross the bridge, look to your right, you'll see a pylon. That's us."

Sometimes at night, we would hear someone clambering over our rusty tin roof and the next day we'd notice new (illegal) wiring, strung from our pylon, stretching over the roofs to someone's shack. Ironically, the poor here (as in most developing countries) pay more for their electricity than the middle-class or rich, simply because they cannot afford the connection fee and so are forced to purchase their electricity through middlemen who charge huge mark-ups.

The second distinguishing feature of our home was a rotting wooden ladder that we had to climb up to get into our house. There were always kids all over the ladder and we quickly came to the realization that our ladder, like most things, was considered public property in the slum. People would laze around on the bottom rung, smoking or chatting, watching people go by or watching us go about our daily lives.

Two years passed living in that house perched at the top of the ladder in Victory Creek Bridge community. And slowly it dawned on me that God was teaching me an important lesson. That ladder was going to become a symbol of my life as a follower of Jesus.

Crunch time came when after a while we noticed that, apart from the local kids who were always keen to come up and play with our toys, not many of our adult neighbors could be bothered climbing up that rickety old ladder to come and visit with us. The novelty had worn off.

We found that if we wanted to build relationships with all our neighbors we would have to climb down our ladder and get down into their homes and lives.

Then one day it struck me that Jesus climbed down the ladder too. Jesus made his descent around 2000 years ago when he walked out of the most exclusive gated community in the universe, setting aside the beauty and splendor of heaven to relocate to earth - amongst us people. When Jesus climbed down the ladder, the "God above us" became Emmanuel—"God with us". The distant and Almighty God of the Old Testament became the alongsider God who walked amongst us.

I must confess to you from the outset that my natural instinct is to do the exact opposite—to climb up the ladder in life, to try to get ahead in the rat race, to compete with my peers in accumulating more and more possessions and to make my life as comfortable and secure as possible. Indeed, before coming to Cambodia I had been a high-flying marketer of computer software, a business in which looking successful was entirely the name of the game. But I had come to see that Jesus modeled a different way. As usual, Jesus was completely counter-cultural—instead of climbing up the ladder, he climbed down the ladder.

And in following Jesus down the ladder I discovered that the incarnational approach works at a number of different levels. I discovered the head, the heart and the hand of incarnation.

The Head

Our incarnational presence had an impact on our community at the head level. We saw, over time, that our neighbors were challenged in their understanding of certain things through their interaction with us.

For example, in Cambodia most people have been exposed to widespread advertising campaigns selling baby milk powder. As a result, almost everyone thinks milk powder is better than breast milk for their babies.[11] Not a huge problem really, unless you are poor. If you are poor like our neighbors you don't have access to clean drinking water. So you mix up dirty water with milk powder and sooner or later your baby gets diarrhea. Not a huge problem unless you are poor. If you are poor like our neighbors, you may not know that a child with diarrhea needs to be rehydrated. If you don't know that, your baby has a good chance of dying of dehydration. So when Nayhouy got pregnant, twice, what better opportunity to be a 'prophetic mother', living out a vital message in the midst of our neighbors. Not that it was all one way of course. They taught us things too, and part our child rearing approach today is also based on what we learnt from our Cambodian friends and neighbors.

But in pregnancy and the early years of raising our kids we were offered a perfect opportunity to engage with our neighbors in a living experiment to see what we could discover together. We decided to feed our daughter Micah nothing but breast milk for the first 6 months of her life: easier, cheaper and much safer. Our neighbors could not believe that we would make this choice. Surely, we would be disadvantaging our children? And so Nayhouy quickly ended up with a bunch of local women watching her progress on an almost daily basis. Since they could observe every aspect of our lives, they knew full well that nothing passed Micah's lips but breast milk.

After six months they were amazed at how healthy and chubby Micah was. And it was all on breast milk. Incredible. We realised that our presence had made a huge difference in their understanding of a life and death issue. A difference that could very well save lives.

The Heart

But incarnation goes right to the heart as well. Sometimes the message that needs to get through is not a cerebral, fact-based or informational thing. Sometimes it's a message straight from the heart. A message of love and value. That was the message my little friend Arit needed to experience.

At thirteen years old, Arit had experienced enough suffering in his short life on the streets to give him a weather-beaten, sun-bleached look. But his eyes were still lively and innocent. He dealt with his bleak existence as a street kid by sniffing glue with a gang of other teenagers in front of our house.[12] He often came to sit with me on our ladder and I would usually end up applying some ointment to some cut or infection he had picked up in the past day or two.

This day was no different. Someone had punched him in the eye hard enough to break the skin and leave him with half his face swollen. As I finished applying the salve, Arit shuffled over to give his gang leader room to sit down with us on the step.

Casually I asked Arit how he came to get this particular wound. "He did it." Arit said with a wry smile, pointing to his leader. To my surprise, the other guy smirked and nodded his concurrence proudly. It took a second to sink in that the guy who was supposed to be Arit's protector on the street had actually inflicted this horrible wound on a little boy. But when it did, I felt a wave of anger sweep over me - I confess I didn't respond with a whole lot of love.

"How could you do that to someone who is supposed to be your friend? Why don't you pick on someone your own size next time - like me?" I ranted, thumb jabbed on chest. Actually I was about a foot taller than this weedy gang leader but I knew he was twice as vicious and wouldn't hesitate to use a knife on me if necessary.

The gang leader didn't take my outburst well. He sneered at me with contempt and spat out a torrent of Cambodian swear words, many of which were new to me. I suppressed my urge to reach for my language notebook to write them down for dissection later with my tutor. In one swift upward motion he was on his feet and sautering away, still cursing me.

A neighbor came and immediately sat in his place, "Why do you even bother with these good-for nothing kids?" he asked incredulously, "Don't you know they are just useless glue-sniffers?" In his eyes, these kids were not worth bothering to talk to, let alone endangering yourself to protect. "Well, the God I follow said that if we receive a child in His name, it's the same as receiving Him" I replied, remembering some of Jesus' words about children. "Jesus loves children, and so must I."

Glancing down with resignation and sadness at Arit, I was surprised to see his face lit up with joy. I realised he didn't care that I was unable to protect him. He didn't mind that I would probably fail in my attempts to get him off the streets and off glue. For him the most important thing was that - perhaps for the first time in his life someone actually cared about him. Someone valued him enough to say so.

The Hand

The natural outworking of a real and deep transformation of the head and the heart will eventually be compassionate service to others. It was at this level that we saw Sarim's transformation occur.

For months Sarim didn't dare to enter our home at Victory Creek Bridge community. It was more than just shyness. Sarim was waiting to see if we could be friends. But when Sarim saw that we weren't going anywhere, that she could trust us, she finally opened up. And one day my wife Nayhouy offered to teach her some English. Sarim jumped at the opportunity.

The relationship developed into a close friendship and Sarim was impacted at both the head and the heart level. As they got to know each other, she became more and more fascinated with this Jesus who loved the poor and gave up his position of comfort to bring good news and healing to them. Eventually Sarim embraced Jesus and dedicated her life to being his follower. But Sarim could see by our lives that being a follower of Jesus was not just a head thing, a cerebral acknowledgement of certain truths. This wouldn't have made sense to her anyway – she was looking for something far more concrete and real than that, something she could touch. But when Sarim discovered that this new 'heart of flesh' she'd received wasn't just for her alone, but something that could spill out through her to touch her whole community - this was a double joy for her. Her new heart had given her a new compassion, and a new sense of vocation.

Sarim had already trained as a nurse, and it wasn't hard for her to team up with other Servants workers and put these skills to work serving the neediest in her community. These days (some six years later) Sarim works full time with TASK, the indigenous Khmer NGO that grew out of Servants work in the slums of Khan Mein Chey (which means 'the Place of Victory'!). She and her co-workers spend their time visiting the homes of children struggling with malnutrition or AIDS, loving them, nursing them and supporting these families in whatever way they can.

Nayhouy and others in Servants and TASK have mentored and discipled her. Sarim has continued to grow in her faith, and in the outworking of that faith, which is compassionate service. A few months ago she was put in charge of this particular child-health project. She prays for the kids and their families and uses her nursing skills to minister to them with Jesus' love. She has become a disciple, walking in the footsteps of Jesus.

By God's grace, and the presence of his followers in the slum, Sarim's life and the lives of many others have been transformed: head, heart and hand.

Meeting Jesus On The Mekong's Edge

Janet Cornwall

(Phnom Penh, Cambodia)

Janet Cornwall, a doctor from New Zealand, arrived in Cambodia in 1995, where she served tirelessly for eleven years among the poorest of the poor. During her time in Phnom Penh, she helped set up the AIDS Home Care, TB and Women's Health ministries, which the TASK staff and local Community Health Workers are now carrying forward.

It was dusk when I got to the small wooden house perched on the river bank. My friend, Mrs Phally, a traditional midwife and one of our neighborhood community health workers, met me at the end of the dirt road, just before it fell away into the swollen brown waters of the the Basaac River, a major Mekong tributary.

One of my most poignant memories of Mrs Phally, who has been a follower of Jesus for almost ten years now, is her bringing to me, nestled in a small box, a tiny stillborn baby, lovingly wrapped in a cloth. The child had been born to a mentally disturbed woman, Ming Navee,[13] who had arrived at our office heavily pregnant and completely deranged. There was no 'official' place that would care for someone like Ming Navee. When Navee arrived, Phally had gently led her back home, and though it was flooded, made her comfortable and tried to help her find some rest. But in the middle of the night Navee went into labour and in her disturbed state began wading into the now deepening flood waters before finally she was pulled back. Mrs Phally found someone with a little boat, and in this way took her down into the local Government health centre. Unimpressed at being disturbed in the night by people of no wealth or status, the medical staff refused to help and sent them away. So Phally took her back in the boat to her home. She delivered the stillborn baby, managed the bleeding, and waited for the morning.

INCARNATION

On this night, Mrs Phally led me through the murky flood waters lapping at our shins until we stepped inside the house. By the light of a tiny kerosene lamp I could see Mrs Sarun lying on a bed under a grubby mosquito net, groaning in pain, vomiting up what little her stomach still contained. We gingerly walked across the planks laid on the dirt floor, now covered in water, climbing up onto the bamboo bed and under the net. Mrs Sarun's husband had died some years before, as had several children. Her remaining son was in prison. She had had abdominal pain for about a year, refusing to go and get help. After all, where would she find the money to pay for medicines anyway? Finally, a few months earlier, she had agreed for Mrs Phally to take her to see the midwife at TASK, the NGO that had sprung out of Servants ministry in the Phnom Penh slums. A referral to a hospital, however, showed that it was too late to do anything about the cancer.

But when I arrived, I did not know any of this background. My assumption was that the younger woman I could see in the other corner of the room was her daughter. After making my examination, as I was leaving, I met a cheerful man, the husband of the younger woman, arriving back home. He was accompanied by a smiling youth who was obviously intellectually impaired. I explained to the man my plan to get some pain relief and other help for his mother. "Oh no", he said, laughing. "That is not my mother. She has no family, but we have been caring for her. And this young man also," he said, indicating the smiling youth. "We are all brothers and sisters in Jesus Christ."

One Sunday morning I was called out into the lane. Ming Sarun, a woman in her early thirties, was clutching her hand, displaying a little finger only attached by a flap of skin, cut as she had raised her hand to stop her husband getting her face with the knife. A few months later she came to me again, this time to show me a lump on her breast, which was obviously a cancer. I referred her to a Christian clinic for surgery and then between us we paid for the best treatment Cambodia has to offer – basic radiotherapy. That bought a few months of comfort.

Shortly after that, I was scheduled to take home-leave and

visit New Zealand for a few weeks. On my return Ming Sarun greeted me at the door, obviously in great distress from the cancer spreading through her body. I gave some medicines and promised to visit her at her home behind the fish factory the next day. She was being cared for by a distant relative on her husband's side, Ming Kuen, who lived with her three young children, husband and frail elderly mother.

To get to the house, I had to wade through raging flood water, which was also the sewerage outflow for all the homes in this small settlement. As I clambered up the rickety ladder and over the bamboo floor, I could see the murky water eddying below. Ming Kuen's middle daughter, about six years old, ran off to fetch her mother from the market where she sold vegetables to support the family. Sarun's pain was no less, and so I arranged to take her out to try and get a place for her in a hospice. As I waded back out through the filthy water and stepped onto the rickety plank bridge that led to drier ground, Ming Kuen followed behind me with a basin. Kneeling down, she filled it with water and washed my feet. My eyes filled with tears, and my Khmer - never that fluent - completely failed me.

Who is incarnating Jesus here on the edge of the Mekong river? Here, where it is a privilege to live, and where forbearance, forgiveness, faithfulness and joy swirl up and around, flooding compassion within, around and through me: tell me, who is incarnating Jesus?

And I pray that you, being rooted and established in love, may have power, together with all the saints, to grasp how wide and long and high and deep is the love of Christ, and to know this love that surpasses knowledge – that you may be filled to the measure of all the fullness of God. (Ephesians 3:17-19)

Broken Dreams: A Journey Into Suffering

Glenn Miles

(Phnom Penh, Cambodia)

Glenn Miles, a nurse from England, and his wife, Siobhan, a physician's assistant from the United States, led the Servants pioneer team into Cambodia in 1993 after spending three and a half years in the refugee camps on the Thai-Cambodia border.

Before leading the first Servants team into Cambodia, I spent several years working in the refugee camps on the Thai-Cambodia border, where wave upon wave of refugees from Pol Pot's gulag dragged themselves to the relative safety of Thailand, arriving malnourished and traumatized after crossing mountains and mine fields to flee the advancing Vietnamese army and the retreating Khmer Rouge.

In the camp I worked with a gifted team and learnt so much, but I also experienced the dissonance of not being able to fully live with the people. We were driven into the camps with walkie-talkies strapped to our side, and at any hint of trouble we were whisked back out by U.N. security, leaving our Cambodian friends behind to face the danger alone – usually artillery shells from the Vietnamese or a shoot out between rival camp factions.

In 1992, after two years of waiting, Servants finally gained the Cambodian Government's permission to enter Cambodia with a health team from all corners of the world. Five trusted Cambodian co-workers from the Thai border camp also returned and joined us, forming the core of what would later become the local Christian NGO TASK.

In Phnom Penh, I moved with my new wife, Siobhan (whom I had met in the refugee camp), into the poor suburb of Chak'en Grey, into a settlement where many local health workers and traditional birth attendants lived. The matriarch of the area (affectionately called *Lok Yay*, or Grandmother) had graciously granted us permission to live there. She would personally come by and check whether Siobhan had cooked the rice properly and generally keep an eye on us.

Not everyone was impressed that we'd come. Some assumed that living in the slums was a form of asceticism, perhaps as a punishment for sins we'd committed in this or a previous life. Some other Christian groups were upset with our approach, accusing us of judging them for living differently. Another secular group accused us of using the incarnational approach as a way of doing sneaky prosetelyzation, and forcing people to believe in Christ. From our incredulous neighbors, the most common response we got was, "If something bad happens you can always leave," which of course was true.

So why did we choose to live in a slum? It wasn't to be martyrs or to flagellate ourselves. We simply wanted to follow Christ by coming down from a high and privileged place to try and live among the poor so we could develop friendships and learn what life was really like for them. And in spite of the challenges, we were grateful to finally be in the place that we felt God had called us to, and with a committed team around us.

After eight months in Cambodia, Siobhan woke with acute abdominal pain, which at first we thought was diarrhea, but then realized was a miscarriage. The air in our room was thick and heavy, the darkness and heat almost suffocating. I pushed opened the doors and windows in an effort to get some air circulating, but this was interpreted as an opportunity for the neighbors to come and see what was happening, and of course they decided they simply had to help. Before long they had found paraffin lamps and candles and some of their midwifery instruments and started trying to "assist" the process. As I was "just a man" they began to push me out of the room, but I insisted on staying and tried hard to fend them off. Seeing Siobhan so vulnerable and bleeding made me feel more helpless than I had ever felt in my life, and I cried out to God to help us.

But in the intensity of the situation and the heat, as the blood pounded through my head and the sweat poured off my face, the room swum and swirled and my legs buckled. I teetered, then fell backwards against a concrete wall, triggering a convulsion that knocked me unconscious, fractured the base of my skull and severed a nerve to my right ear, causing immediate deafness.

Meanwhile, Siobhan was lying on her back, bleeding, having lost our longed for first baby in the middle of a slum, in the middle of the night, during curfew, in a country which at that time had a totally non-functional health system while I was unconscious and severely injured.

Yet when we look back, we continue to be amazed by the determination and care of our Cambodian neighbors and friends. In spite of the curfew they managed to get us across town to our team's retreat house. And even though we had only been with them for months, they wept with us when it was clear we would have to leave the country. We truly felt that we had entered their lives and become members of their community.

The team gathered around us and prayed with us and for us, as did the broader Christian community in Phnom Penh, who then mobilized a network of people around the world to help and pray. After two weeks in Bangkok, we were able to finally get a flight back to the U.K, where we were taken to one of the most prestigious private hospitals in London, usually reserved for Arab princes and movie stars! One day we were eating rice in a slum and shortly afterwards, we were eating gourmet food from a five-star menu.

Over that first year, as we tried to come to terms with so many losses—the baby, my disability, our future—and I tried to cope with the pounding head pain and severe bouts of nerve pain in my face, I became depressed. We didn't know what the future held for us – was it to return to Cambodia, or not? My hearing impairment remained, and I had lost a lot of capacity since the accident.

When Siobhan became pregnant again, we were a bit surprised, since we had hoped to get a little more stable first, and I was still not able to work. On the due date, Siobhan realized she was bleeding—we later learned that the placenta had come away from the womb—and after being rushed to the hospital in an ambulance, our daughter, Zoe, was born by emergency caesarian section. Two years later, we became pregnant again, and during the final stages of pregnancy, there were complications, and we nearly lost our precious Hannah.

When Tearfund, one of the largest Christian charities in Britain, offered me a job focusing on vulnerable children, I accepted it, but wondered why we were still in Britain. Had we misunderstood what we thought was God's call on us for Cambodia? Then, after several months, Tearfund invited us to apply for a position as the 'Children at Risk Facilitator' in Cambodia. After all that we'd been through, it seemed that our dream might die and we might never get back to Cambodia. But we never gave up, and neither does God.

Seven years after leaving, we returned to Cambodia, but with our two children and my new role, we did not feel we could live in a slum again. We understood that life had changed for us, and accepted that God had a new place for us. We prayed for and were happy to find a wooden house where both our Cambodian friends and expatriate colleagues could feel comfortable visiting us.

Much of our second year was spent in torturous negotiations with various ministries of the Cambodian Government as we tried to adopt our baby, Sarah Nayhouy. The "delivery" of each of our children has been very complicated, and this one was no different! There were months of going from one department to another to get endless forms signed and delivered. Then, the day after the ceremony, in which Sarah was handed over to us to be her parents, the adoption was revoked with the explanation that Siobhan was American. (An American moratorium on adoptions had begun and the Cambodian Government was angry with President Bush.) Eventually, after more anxious months of prayer and paperwork, we finally had full custody of Sarah, and a sense that our family was complete.

After five years back in Cambodia, we sensed that God was calling us to return to Britain to pursue further study and training. Towards the end of our time, we were thrilled to be present at the ceremony when Servants Cambodia handed over the baton of leadership to the locally formed TASK organization. So much of what I had once dreamed of seeing had now come to pass in the healing ministries of these amazing Cambodian men and women. Their work with the AIDS patients, orphans, malnourished and disabled kids in the Mein Chey district shine like a beacon in these slums. And though we were only able to play a small part in the process of getting it all started, God cradled the seed and kept it growing. It was his dream, and he never allowed it to be extinguished.

We left Cambodia knowing that there were many able and inspired Cambodian co-workers, both in TASK and in Tearfund, who would carry on the dream God has for healing the people of this beautiful nation.

Finding God In Beauty And Brokenness

Joshua Palma

(Manila, Philippines)

Joshua Palma is a Filipino who spent much of his life living and working on Smokey Mountain, the infamous rubbish dump on which thousands of Manila's poorest lived. Now, Joshua is a part of the Philippines Servants team and works with other urban poor leaders to realize their dreams for their communities and for their own lives.

Bridging the Gap

I grew up in an evangelical Christian family, hearing story after story of people in the Bible talking to and hearing directly from God—Moses, Samuel, David, Paul and all the rest. I always wanted that to be my experience too.

I have had so many times in my life when I desperately wanted – needed—to talk to and hear God directly. I was struggling with hard questions and needed clear answers. Many times I was at crisis point. A few years ago I had fallen in love with a girl and wanted to ask her to marry me. But was this real love, and was marriage right for me? Then, almost simultaneously, I lost my job and couldn't find another one, no matter how hard I tried. Everything was falling apart. *Why? What should I do?* My heart cried out for God to speak to me, but I heard no voice, no answer.

A year later, I found myself living on Smokey Mountain, Manila's infamous garbage dump. Once more I found myself falling in love, this time not with a girl, but with the poor of this whole community. A rich courage and humor permeated their struggle for daily survival, and it swept me off my feet. And I'm still in love with the people of that poor community.

A few more years passed, and then I found myself transported across land and sea, far from the humid slums of Manila to the snow-capped peaks of Switzerland. I had been asked to speak about my life, and the life of Manila's urban poor to the people in the churches of Switzerland. *Oh God,* I begged, *what am I supposed to say? What on earth am I doing in a rich place like sweet, beautiful Switzerland? How can I make any sense of all that I am experiencing?* Like a fish out of water, I had no words to describe what I saw and felt. Once more I desperately wanted to talk to and hear from God. I went alone to the woods. I wanted to cry, but no tears fell from my eyes. I could not hear God. All I could hear were the birds singing and the noise of a brook rushing over broken stones. After I left the woods, I had three strange encounters with three elderly Swiss women. I knew God sent them to me, and through each of them I heard God's voice.

The first I saw from afar. She was so old and frail, so skinny and wrinkled, barely just skin and bones. I asked myself: is she really so different from all the old women I know and love in my poor community on Smokey Mountain?

The second I met as we both stood looking out of the ferry's window at the azure blue of Lake Zurich. She had heard me speak at a church meeting and tried hard to strike up a conversation with me, but I didn't speak Swiss, and she didn't speak English.

In her beautiful, wrinkle-encompassed eyes, I saw a desperation to bridge the gap between our languages, our nationalities, our richness and poverty. Finally, she put her mouth close to my ear and whispered: "I love you!"

The third woman, I had met before, and I knew her by name. She was very sick and would probably die soon. She spoke about Jesus and about her struggle to face death, simply and without pretense. I looked into her eyes and they were mirrors; I saw myself, and a life both so beautiful and so ugly. I felt myself losing control, and my tears began to fall abundantly. Nothing else in this world mattered anymore. I wanted to live for Jesus and the poor until the last breath of my life.

Afterwards, in the silence, Jesus was speaking to me: "Don't expect me to always speak dramatically like I did with Moses, Samuel and Paul." I realized there never was a time when He was not speaking to me. He was speaking to me, and His words were sinking into me, being absorbed and silently becoming part of my being.

And I will know how well I have been listening by how well I have loved the poor and the struggling ones He sends across my path. In the cool, rich grandeur of Switzerland, I heard God's call on my life spoken clearly, beckoning me to go back and serve Him amongst the warmth of the beautiful Philippines and among the beautiful, broken lives of the urban poor

Transformation: The Other Side of the Story

Nervously I forced myself to step into the beautiful, spacious hall owned by an affluent and "successful" church congregation for a gathering of religious people involved in development work. Many with a reputation for their sterling work on behalf of the poor were there. Some I even knew from Smokey Mountain, my community made 'famous' by the huge hill of rotting garbage upon which I and my neighbors lived and worked everyday. Curiosity and a passion to learn had eventually overcome my anxieties about coming to this meeting in the richest part of town, where I just didn't feel like I belonged. But two dear Swiss friends, a husband and wife who were Servants workers living in a neighboring squatter area, had convinced me to come. "We should at least try and stay up to date with what the powerful movers and shakers in development are doing and saying," they had argued. We were also drawn by the forum's title: "A successful model of transforming Smokey Mountain."

The food served around was not too elaborate, and the quantity only slightly more than was needed. The host church's ladies group was taking charge elegantly and dutifully, mingling and making sure that everybody had enough. I cynically wondered if they—along with so many other middle-class seminary graduates working for the poor—were being careful because they had just read Ronald Sider's much assigned *Rich Christians in an Age of Hunger*.

I was starting to feel rebellious as I silently questioned the choice of venue for this forum. If Smokey Mountain really is in the process of being transformed into a new heaven and a new earth, why were we not having the celebration there, with the Smokey Mountain people all participating too?

Of course there were selected representatives from Smokey Mountain strategically placed up on the stage, giving excellent performances and inspiring speeches, each rewarded with enthusiastic applause from the crowd. I found myself staring at the floor, afraid to look directly into their eyes as I realized that I hardly knew any of them. Had I become a stranger on Smokey Mountain, completely out of touch with life in my own community?

A male European theologian noted for his development thinking stood and talked about how respect for local religious figures and traditions had been the key instrument in the transformation of Smokey Mountain. The Filipino lady who chaired the forum hailed the dawn of two mainstream religions working together for the sake of the poor, and so overcoming their perennial theological differences. The spirit of ecumenism was in the air. Everybody was applauding so appreciatively, except my Swiss friend, who had walked out of the room during a speech from one of those well-known Smokey Mountain religious figures.

Though I was impressed by the eloquence of the speeches and surprised at how the crowd was captivated, I began to feel trapped and unsure of how I should behave. I wished I had walked out with my friend, but now it was too late. I didn't want to attract attention to myself, and already I was feeling terribly self-conscious, sure that those who knew about my involvement with Smokey Mountain were glancing at me, watching my reaction, knowing that if I were to speak about life on Smokey Mountain, I would be telling a different story.

The big speeches and presentations were so moving that I sometimes found myself joining in with the crowd's applause. Then I would catch myself and stop, wishing I didn't know the other side of the story. In the end, I walked out of the church hall feeling defeated, with the last thread of my trust in the big religious establishments broken. I also felt guilty for not walking out earlier with my friend, but because she is Swiss, she can afford to be blunt. I'm a poor Filipino and have to be polite. My feelings swirled around and around in my heart. Anger, guilt, embarrassment.

Outside the hall, the tables were laden with fundraising brochures from prominent religious organizations—elites that obviously led the way not only in development thinking, but also the business of fundraising. Though the brochures had been few and discrete before the presentations, now they shone shamelessly like neon advertisements.

In that pathway outside that church hall of the rich, I could not help thinking about the people of Smokey Mountain enduring hunger and despair after their shanty homes had been razed by Government demolition crews, while the holy and informed celebrated a "transformational work" well done. I wondered what God was feeling on that day when bullets and tear gas were sprayed across Smokey Mountain, followed by bulldozers and sledgehammers. Was He sharing this self-congratulatory euphoria, satisfied that an answer had been given to some developmentalist's prayer?

I left the beautiful church and its tables of fundraising materials and went searching for my Swiss friend, needing to be with someone

31

who understood. My steps were uncertain and my legs unsteady, numbed by confused emotions. An outrageous desire entered my heart: to go back and overturn those tables.

But I was not Jesus. I was simply a poor Filipino from Smokey Mountain.

A Jewel Worth Noticing

Our slum was almost denied the chance to celebrate our first 'World Eradication of Poverty Day' when the Quezon City Government refused us permission to use the local Catholic Shrine, telling us that our activity *"was not appropriate to the sanctity of that holy place."* We searched for alternative venues only to be turned down several times more. It seemed that neither the rich nor the middle-class had any room in their inns for the birthing of our rag-tag idea. On top of all this, we all had busy lives and ministries in our respective slum communities, leaving us meager time and energy for organizing this celebration.

Finally, we asked a friend—who had grown up in the slum community, improved his economic situation, but chosen to stay there—to take over the organization of the event. Though he could have moved out of the slum with his family, he saw something deeply precious in the life of his community, something of infinite worth at its heart, a jewel few others ever notice.

On the day of the event, many people arrived from our urban poor communities, churches and the network of ministries that permeated them, sitting on chairs we provided or watching from their shanties nearby. A group of Christian young people from *Payatas* (the largest garbage-dump community in Manila) were scheduled to perform an ethnic dance in our program, but they were stranded on Commonwealth Avenue because the motorcade surrounding the President of the United States had caused gridlock on the main roads. While we were struggling to hold our little community celebration, George Bush was on his way to meet with the rich and the powerful of our land, urging Filipinos to be the "light of Asia and beyond."

Every now and then, choppers that formed part of President Bush's security flew overhead, as if to remind us that we were a tiny bunch of nobodies doing little things in hidden corners of the city. When we started preparing the snacks, children eagerly came to help, pushing, shoving, laughing. One small girl, frustrated at her inability to push to the front of the queue, put her bare foot in one of the empty juice boxes and scuffed away. Soon every kid was skidding around wearing these substitute skates, and the basketball court was transformed into a rink! When you are poor, imagination is the only tool you have to help you enjoy the same games other children take for granted.

The young people who were stranded on Commonwealth Avenue arrived just in time to perform their dance, and the celebration culminated with symbols of hope as the large crowd broke into small groups to discuss their dreams and prayers for a better society yet to come. Afterwards, all the participants drew their visions onto a large white banner edged with ethnic designs: the *Telon Ng Pag-asa*, which literally means 'a widescreen of hope'. After drawing their dreams on the banner the participants each cut a piece from its edge to take home as a symbol and a remembrance.

Though still aware of our smallness, we packed up with contented hearts that day, knowing we had made a statement to our community, our networks, and ourselves. We had dreamed of a better world. We had sown seeds of hope.

What Is The Church?

Dorothy Mathieson

(Manila, Philippines)

Dorothy Mathieson, a pastor, was in Manila and Bangkok with Servants for several years from the late 1980s. Following that she served as the Australian Servants Coordinator and the Servants International Coordinator from 2000 to 2003. Presently she and her husband George minister to overseas students in Brisbane, Australia, and train people in the use of TESOL (Teaching English to Speakers of Other Languages) for use in cross-cultural mission.

One of the biggest challenges I faced in sharing with other Christians about our work among the poor was their piercing and obviously 'meant-to-be corrective' question: "but... are you planting churches?" When I was with Servants in Manila, we had decided that it would be better for us to support and encourage existing fellowships rather than take the easier route (in the Philippines) of starting our own churches.[14] But that frequent question from others in the missionary community seemed to be suggesting that no matter what cooperative network or transformative venture we initiated in a slum, there would be something badly lacking if we had not planted our own church. As I am personally deeply committed to the growth and health of God's church, this question always challenged me. But it also caused me to ask yet deeper questions – "yes, but what is the church? *Who* should be the planter? And *what* will it look like in a slum?"

The slum where I lived in Manila was called Welfareville. It was so named as it was next door to a huge asylum, and it was somehow assumed that the "welfare" of that place would spill over onto the thousands of desperately poor families in the surrounding community. Some local Christians in my community had also come to believe that not just benevolence, but also evil spirits, were spilling over into Welfareville from that asylum. They always hurried past trees in the area, figuring that those spirits dwelt in the trees and would plop down on anyone careless enough to linger in their shade. They claimed that many an unfortunate soul had ended up 'possessed' in this way. To me this belief (and the resulting avoidance of shade) seemed very impractical in such a hot place. In fact, despite all my training in contextualization and cross-cultural sensitivity, I just couldn't bring myself to agree with them. Maybe I'd received *too much* theological training!

They had a church that met in a tin shed. When the temperatures soared I used to wish we could meet under a tree. But we had to swelter instead. Before the service a church troop traveled through the slum beating a drum "to chase the devil and spirits away." I hid in my house as they went by. Being committed to supporting and encouraging the local fellowship in my community sounded great on paper, but was excruciating in practice.

Services were loud and late and long. As the worship progressed people would shake and cry continuously. I was embarrassed and prayed for order and peace (and for the service to end and for nobody to notice that I was linked with this group). I must admit a great passion started to rise up in me to plant a "decent" church. In fact, one day I tried to model a more appropriate style of evangelism by holding a street party in my neighborhood. Of course the church members came too—and stood at the door and ripped off guests' wrist cords worn to protect them from these evil spirits from the asylum. They wrecked my attempt to show a softer form of evangelism! Now everybody knew I was one of *them*.

One Sunday morning I was again at worship, reluctant, questioning and getting fed up. Everyone else was shaking and crying. Even the local dogs seemed to join in. Then a blind woman was led into the middle of all of this. Someone bravely called out, "Sister Dorothy will now pray for Sister Rosalio to see!" (Well yes, theologically I agreed – we were all sisters, but I really didn't know if I wanted to be included in this particular family act...). This invitation deeply embarrassed me, but there didn't seem to be any way out. I mumbled some sort of prayer while the shaking and crying and singing swelled all around me. But my emotions were swirling in a different direction. How could they offer false hope to a woman who had suffered blindness for over twenty years? They were heaping suffering upon suffering! I was angry for Rosalio, but also for myself – I was about to be shown up as inadequate despite all my training and ministry track record. I didn't like what was happening, but had nothing better to suggest or offer. The "worship" continued for ages. Then another call came, "Sister

Rosalio, tell us what color blouse Sister Dorothy is wearing." Rosalio called out, "Red!" And she was right.

My church would have been more theologically ordered. I would have planted a decent church. But probably Sister Rosalio would still be blind.

No Words

Ruth Cooke

(Aceh, Indonesia)

Ruth Cooke is a community nurse with experience in New Zealand and Canada. She spent early 2005 and late 2006 in Aceh province with a Servants health team that entered the area following the tsunami, where she helped develop a community health curriculum for schools and then trained teachers to deliver it.

As I take in the destruction of the homes and villages of Banda Aceh and surrounding villages, I am dumbstruck as I try to imagine the thousands of bodies that lined the streets on the day of the tsunami. It is easy to do when you look at the remains of a house and see a child's toy where a bedroom may have been, or a woman's shoe near the front door. Was the child clutching the toy as he was swept away by a torrent of water? Was the woman wearing that shoe as she tried to escape? Was there someone in that car that is wrecked so badly I can only recognise the steering wheel? There are no words, it seems, to describe the complete devastation surrounding me. Any I can think of are too trite to portray the pain and loss caused by what many have called "the worst natural disaster in the world."

INCARNATION

What do I say to a man I meet who cries as he tells me he was "lucky" enough to be away from his home in Aceh that Boxing Day Sunday, December 26, 2004, when at a few minutes past 8 a.m., a huge earthquake struck just off the western coast of the island of Sumatra, triggering a tsunami. Waves up to thirty meters in height and traveling at six hundred kilometers an hour washed over his home, even though it was located three kilometers away from the beach. When he arrived in his suburb, he was horrified to find a ship the size of a football field sitting on top of his home and the homes of his neighbors. All around him was a scene of total destruction – mud, water, debris, car wreckages and the bodies of friends and neighbors who had perished. Even worse than not being able to find his home, he could not find his family. Three months after the day of devastation, he assumes that his wife and children remain underneath the huge tonnage of ship that is impossible to shift off his home. What can I say to give him comfort?

What do I say to an eight-year-old child who has lost her mother and father, three siblings and her home in a beach side village near Banda Aceh? She is brought to me by a teacher for medicine for skin infections she has had since the tsunami. She doesn't smile. What can I possibly do to ease her grief?

What can I say to leaders in this community, where I am working to provide medical relief for those affected by the loss of loved ones, housing, and basic needs of shelter, water, clothing and nutrition. All the children in the school I am working in have at least one parent dead. Twenty-five percent of them are completely orphaned. Twelve hundred lives were lost in this community alone. I know how I feel when one person I know dies. I can't comprehend the depths of their grief and despair. How do I tell them I am sorry for their loss?

What do I say to the woman who has come to see me with her daughter, who cries with tears of grief and gratitude, thanking me for coming from so far away to help?

I ask God, *why*? *Why* did all the children in a primary school die that Sunday morning at 8 a.m. as they were swallowed by a giant wave? *Why* did all the patients in one hospital perish as mud engulfed them while they lay in their sick beds? *Why* are 170,000 men, women or children dead or presumed dead in Aceh alone because of this disaster? I still don't know the answers.

What I do know is that God sent me to be *with* the people of Aceh. I don't know what to say and have no words of comfort I can give them. But I want to tell them that God loves and cares for them, and the only way I know how to do that is by being with them as they rebuild their lives and communities. We struggle together, to find meaning and hope amidst the pain. As we do this in partnership, I learn so much about God's heart for His people.

A translator I have been working with wrote me this poem:

Tell your people there,
your husband, your family, your neighbors, your relatives,
that the Achenese thank you so much -
using their grief, their sadness and their hopes.
Sometimes we don't need tears to express our grief;
Sometimes we don't need laughter or smiles
to describe our happiness—
because we do not have tears or smiles left to express everything
we felt while our lovely people passed away in front of our eyes.
Don't try to teach us how to cry.
But let's learn together how to smile again, despite our grief.
Thank you so much for your sacrifice for our people.

As I leave the province of Aceh, I will take with me many memories. Many of them will be sad memories, but the memories that will stay the longest are the sounds of Aceh: the sounds of saws and hammers as people rebuild, and the sound of children's laughter as they learn to play and be children again. These are the sounds of resilience.

I feel very privileged to have been involved in the lives of these people who have taught me so much. I am grateful to be even a small part of their story.

What will I say when I am back in New Zealand and my family, friends and work colleagues ask how my time was in Aceh? How will I respond when a co-worker asks if I enjoyed my "holiday." How will I tell them about the friends I made, the lives I've been touched by, the extreme devastation and trauma that surrounded me, the work that filled my days here. Once again, I will find that I have no words. Only love.

Floating In Faith

Steve Tripp

(Aceh, Indonesia)

Steve Tripp is a doctor from New Zealand, who helped lead the initial Servants health team into Banda Aceh following the tsunami. (With the completion of the relief phase there, Servants has since transferred their efforts from Aceh to Jakarta, with a long term urban poor team beginning there late 2009). Steve, Wendy, and their family are now members of the Servants team in Phnom Penh, Cambodia.

My eyes sweep over the partially demolished houses surrounded by rubble, mud and tracks from the numerous trucks and heavy machinery that pass every few minutes. Kilometer after kilometer with almost nothing standing more than a meter off the ground. It just didn't seem real. A moonscape.

A flat bottomed barge, larger in length and width than an Olympic swimming pool, was picked up by the sea and deposited three kilometres inland as if it were a baby laid in a cot. Nearby stands a mosque with its white walls shining and its dome glowing in defiance of the distortion surrounding it. Those on the ship were the lucky ones. No one will ever know how many lie beneath it.

Tens of thousands were killed soon after waking up for a normal day. A concrete pad with a car pit signals the position of a mechanical workshop. Were they already at work for the day? Was there someone in that car pit? It's the small things that touch you the most: a broken sandal, a bent kitchen fork, a toilet brush, an iron. I pick up a broken computer CD. In English I read the title of a computer game my own child has played. Who played this game here? Was it a girl or a boy? Am I standing on his or her grave? Walking on a cemetery? The ship is to remain as a memorial to those who died in the tsunami, lest we forget. And at one end of the ship, in a vertical space of less than half a meter, a banana tree grows, providing a glimpse of the new life that grows even after such destruction.

We walk through what may have been a police housing area—a concrete foundation, tiles. Parts of brick walls are strewn everywhere. Nothing standing above half a meter off the ground except a toilet.

At the shore, looking inland, I see a wasteland stretching for three kilometers. Beside us stands the remains of seven-meter lighthouse. The top, including the light, has been completely removed. Facing the sea, I can see the foundations of what used to be a civic building thirty meters off-shore.

Seeing the devastation, I feel sad, awestruck, and incredulous, as well as a heightened awareness of our common humanity— Aceh and Kiwi, Muslim and Christian, in all our fragility, stupidity, strength, creativity, and resourcefulness. This didn't happen to "them", it happened to "us".

Driving along, I pass a wall with graffiti scrawled in Indonesian, recognize the words "Allah'" and "Tsunami." Many of us have asked questions of God. Part of the shared human experience is to ask questions. I ask, *What now? What can I do?*

My first answer is, *write it down*. Record it. This must not be forgotten. I must not let myself grow numb to tragedy. Becoming desensitized to tragedy is becoming less human. If anything good can come out of this or any other disaster, let it be that we grow in a sense of shared humanity, that we open our eyes, our minds, our hearts to the rest of the world, that we learn to live for each other.

I have walked on a peoples' graves. I have seen the devastation and now I have the privilege and responsibility of being here as just another drop in the bucket. We can't just ask questions. We—all of us—must seek to be the answer.

When my tour of duty is over, and I have used up all the leave I could squeeze out of my employer, I have to leave this upside down place and return to the 'stability' of New Zealand. I feel sad to be leaving, but happy to be going home; fulfillment for what has been achieved, but also a sense that I am leaving unfinished work, a story without an ending. I came in faith, believing God had called me to do this. Now I leave, trusting that God will do something with the work we started. But there's no way of knowing if what I have sacrificed here will make any difference, if there will be people and resources available to continue our efforts. But "faith is being sure of what we hope for and certain of what we do not see" (Hebrews 11:1).

On my last morning before leaving Aceh, while sleeping in a guest house set aside for relief workers, I was woken at 5 a.m. by Islamic prayer calls outside my tent. After a half an hour, as the prayers wound down, some Christians started up with their praise music—the same ones who had been at it until midnight the night before! Just as I was dropping back to sleep at 6:30, I felt the unmistakable motion of an earthquake, which gave me the feeling of floating, as if sitting on my surfboard just beyond the break.

We live on tectonic plates and are always floating on the surface of the earth. We spend so much of our time, money and energy trying to gain control over the world around us, trying to gain security over our own destiny, trying to build our towers of Babel. When will we learn to seek harmony with our world, to move when she moves, to sway when she sways? Why do we try to overpower and subdue our planet? Why do we keep coming up against each other in conflict? We are simply walking on water, floating on a sea of lava. When will we learn to seek harmony with God, and to move when he moves?

It's not an easy thing, this learning to trust, to float, this realization that I'm not in control, that I need to choose to submit each day to the creator of this living planet.

Wounded Healers:
Concluding Reflections On Incarnation

Kristin Jack

Yes, the world is full of suffering...but
also of the overcoming of suffering.

Helen Keller

Deng was one of the first neighbors we got to know when we moved into our first slum in 1994. Having grown up as an orphan with almost no schooling, Deng could barely read. As a new Christian, she once pulled a knife on another woman during an argument in our small group meeting—something we didn't see often during our Bible study groups back in New Zealand! Deng had married a rogue of a husband who was away from home for long periods of time as he looked for work. Sometimes Deng and he would quarrel, and blows would be struck. But over the years that we knew Deng, the "diamond" within her was smoothed and polished by the love of Christ. Miraculously, her husband eventually gave his life to Christ, and his drinking and gambling stopped, the fights stopped, and, perhaps for the first time, Deng found human love. Before meeting Jesus, Deng's husband had contracted HIV/AIDS and Deng contracted it from him.

Over time, Deng and her husband grew very weak and sick, but as far as Deng was concerned, she still had good news to share, because she had found Jesus, who loved her and treasured her. In the last two years of her life, Deng brought fourteen of her neighbors to faith in Christ. Even while she was dying, she was more alive than a lot of people with better 'health'. She had found real life, and nothing—not even her own suffering—was going to stop her from sharing that with others.

Savath is another old friend of ours, who these days manages TASK's project HALO caring for children orphaned by AIDS. He once told me how he'd come to follow Jesus. Like so many others, he'd fled the Pol Pot regime as the Vietnamese were invading in 1979-80, and made it to one of the many refugee camps set up just inside the Thai border. In this particular camp, an evangelical Christian group were active in running public health programs, and they had recruited Savath to help them. Every lunch time, Savath's co-worker, a zealous young western nurse, tried to engage Savath in a Bible study. But as Savath recalled those Bible studies for me, he smiled ruefully: "I found them so boring and pointless. They just didn't make any sense to me." And so he would do everything he could to avoid them. After awhile his co-worker gave up on the Bible studies, sensing that they were pushing Savath further away rather than drawing him closer. But she asked Savath to help her identify and visit the poorest and most disadvantaged families in the camp so that the health team could provide extra care for them. As he visited people, everything he'd heard about in the Bible studies began to make sense. Jesus. Love. The poor. Compassion. Salvation. Grace. And Savath could see that he had a place in it all: God had something useful for him to do, something beautiful to offer his community. He was discovering a sense of vocation.

Henri Nouwen writes that those of us who follow Jesus are, like him, wounded healers. It is really only those who have suffered—like Joshua Palma or Glenn and Siobhan Miles, or Savath —who can reach out with genuine empathy to those who are suffering. It is our own experience of pain that enables us to experience real compassion for others in pain. Those who cruise through life somehow avoiding tragedy end up living very shallow lives indeed, and have little of substance to offer others. The identity of "wounded healer" truly describes Jesus, our crucified Messiah— he who was "despised and rejected by men, a man of sorrows, familiar with suffering"; and it truly describes those who seek to follow him.

But God does not allow us to know suffering simply in order to crush us or destroy us. When offered back to him, our suffering—as Deng so beautifully taught Susan and I — can be transformed into love, compassion and deeper service. And thus we are transformed into new people. People who know the crucified Messiah – and the risen Lord.

Within Servants, we are fond of saying that ministry should spring out of relationships rather than programs. And in Craig's story about climbing down the ladder—a great metaphor for incarnational mission—this was what Sarim was looking for. She wanted to know if Craig and Nayhouy could genuinely be her friends, and part of that was knowing they would be around for a long time. We do a great damage when we separate out the head, heart and hand aspects of the gospel and exalt one part over the others. But this is just what so much Christianity has done down through the ages, with its over-emphasis on doctrines and creeds on the one hand, and what Dietrich Bonhoeffer called "cheap grace" (or easy believism), on the other. But many people – people like Sarim and Savath – are thirsty, waiting for the Word to become flesh and dwell amongst them. As Ruth Cooke and Steve Tripp demonstrate in their moving accounts from Aceh, Indonesia after the tsunami, perhaps the simplest – and best – definition of incarnational ministry is this: "if you see someone hurting, get your body there."

A Body Out of Shape

Kristin Jack

Lord it seems to me
your body is all out of shape
and the world stares aghast
at this malformed oaf
denouncing so much
with its huge lips
obscuring the heart.

We teeter on tiny legs
staggering
from judgment to scandal
gesticulating wildly
as lives slip from our too few hands.

Lord, it seems to me
your gospel has too many mouths
and too few legs,
too many talking heads
swollen with self-importance,
and not enough hands
blistered from touching the pain
of a world bent on self-immolation.

Lord, it seems to me
your church has too many men
wearing suits and ties
when a laborer's shirt is what's needed,
so many execs in black shiny shoes
when your sandals were frayed
and dust caked from walking;
and Lord, it seems to me
your rescue effort is staffed
by too many women with microphone-lapels
when the tools that you gave us
were the basin and the towel.

1. Michka Assayas, Bono on Bono (Hodder and Stoughton, 2005), 125.
2. John 20:21-22.
3. Henri Nouwen, Gracias!, (Orbis books, 1983), p147-148
4. John 1:14, The Message.
5. John 14:7-9.
6. Philippians 2:5-11.
7. e.g., John 5:19.
8. 1 John 4:7-12, 16.
9. 1 John 3:16-18.
10. Philippians 3:10-11.
11. Our team mate, Susan Jack, was later involved in a campaign to have milk powder advertising banned in Cambodia.
12. In Phnom Penh alone, there are an estimated 10,000 street kids, many of whom are addicted to glue or harder drugs.
13. Throughout the book, some of the names have been changed to protect confidentiality.
14. In fact, Servants had previously planted a number of churches in the slums of Manila. These Living Springs churches have all been handed over completely to Filipino leadership and control, and they continue to grow and minister wholistically to their communities.

Two

COMMUNITY

You say you care about the poor. Then
tell me, what are their names?

Gustavo Gutierrez[1]

INTRODUCTION: WHAT ARE THEIR NAMES?

Kristin Jack

Receive Onesimus back forever, not as a slave, but more than as a
slave... as a dear friend...a person ...and as a follower of the Lord.
(Philemon 15-16).

Mother Teresa once said that though the poverty of the East may be more visible, the poverty of the West – loneliness – is also deadly. Knowing this, we make the commitment to work with people, not just for them. To paraphrase Bishop Leslie Newbigen, Jesus never wrote a book nor tract nor magazine, nor appeared on TV nor radio. Jesus never built a Bible school nor a college, nor started an NGO nor a church. Instead

He founded a community of disciples: and it was by this that he turned the world upside down. Therefore, we too have a passion to work together in supportive teams that model the love, care and community of which Jesus spoke.

In this section on Community, you will hear stories from Servants workers who have struggled with the inadequacy that so often prevents us from getting involved in the lives of others, especially in the lives of the poor. But instead of treating 'the poor' (or 'the lost') as a category for professionals and experts to 'deal' with, they have responded by embracing the people they encounter as sacred individuals with unique dreams, hopes and histories. Instead of being paralyzed by the insecurities that plague us - "What can I offer them? What skill, resource or advice can I give that will alleviate their poverty and their pain?" - they have simply chosen to love their neighbors as themselves.

You will read about one Servants worker in India who took the risk of moving into a strange new community, befriending three of his neighbors, spending time with them, learning their language and their culture, making himself vulnerable, and sharing the most precious thing he had in his life: his friendship with Jesus. Through that transforming relationship, one young Indian man came to love those whom he'd previously held in indifference - the poorest in his community - and to reject the casteism that still plagues India, despite Gandhi's best efforts. Though he was often overwhelmed by feelings of great sadness as he witnessed the desperate lives of the people around him, the Holy Spirit led him to build relationships of trust with a few of his neighbors, gradually explaining his beliefs in response to their genuine curiosity, all the while praying for the Spirit to reveal God's love to those who had become his dear friends.

In another story, you will read about one young teenager stranded in the concrete and asphalt jungle of Metro Manila in the Philippines who was "found" by Servants workers who loved him when he was restless and driven by drug addiction and fear of death. Their unconditional love eventually drew him to the feet of Jesus, where he discovered self-worth and dignity and over time became a trustworthy leader at a drug rehab camp for street youth.

As Mick Duncan (who led the Servants team in Manila from 1987 through 1992) discovered when he risked looking foolish in his early days of Filipino language learning: "What I had to offer my neighbors was the gift of my own weaknesses and vulnerability."[2]

Our friend Ash Barker in UNOH says that we can't chant the phrase "make poverty history" until we have first learnt how to "make poverty personal". We think he is right. In all of the stories collected here, you will hear about Servants workers developing relationships of genuine friendship and trust with the neighbors they have the privilege and joy of knowing. Central to the Servants' principle of 'community' is the conviction that the most effective way to share the Gospel of Christ with others is never through programs and projects, but from heart to heart through the medium of compassionate hands, listening ears, and lovingly honest lips, from one vulnerable human being to another.

Remembering Richard

Mick Duncan

(Manila, Philippines)

Mick Duncan, a Pastor from New Zealand, and his wife, Ruby, arrived in Manila in the mid-1980s and led the Servants Team there from 1987 to 1992.

We will never forget our first Christmas Eve in the slum, waking to the sound of rocks clattering onto our flimsy corrugated iron roof. Peeping outside I saw the gang of drunken men responsible for the mayhem. Ruby and I gathered up the children and huddled together in a secure corner of our new home. Quietly I prayed that one day I would make personal contact with one of the gang members and see him come to Christ.

One day, while toiling away at language learning by hitting the streets every day to practice a few short sentences, I managed to corner two unsuspecting boys.

"Ano ang mga pangalan ninyo?" I stammered out, clumsily asking for their names. They dutifully informed me that they were Richard and Boyet.

"At saan kayo nakatira ngayon?" I asked. In response, they pointed out where they lived. So far so good!

"At, saan kayo papunta?" I inquired. They indicated the general direction they were going by pointing with their lips, something I had learned was culturally more polite than pointing a finger.

Having exhausted my entire Filipino vocabulary to date, I simply stood in front of the boys and smiled awkwardly. After much shuffling of feet, I said, *"Sige,"* (okay) and walked off, feeling very much like a two-year-old.

Two months later, while still laboring away at language learning, I caught a glimpse of Richard about to turn into an alley about three hundred meters away.

"Hi Richard!" I yelled. He looked back in my direction with shock and surprise, then disappeared around the corner.

Some months later, there was a knock on our flimsy plywood door. When I opened it, I found Richard standing before me. I greeted him and asked what he wanted in Filipino.

"A bible study," he said.

"Come right on in," I said, opening the door.

Richard came knocking at our door again and again over the next several months, and during our time together, I would point to an English verse and he would locate it in a Filipino Bible. In between reading Scripture together, I also learned Richard's sad story: how his parents had split up and deserted him and his six siblings when he was fifteen; how they lived together in a damp hole in the ground; and how Richard ran with a gang of thieves to feed them.

One day, to my shock and surprise, he blurted out, *"I've become a follower of Jesus."*

"What did it for you?" I asked, struggling to understand his conversion to Christ, since I didn't think our Bible studies had been that great.

"One day," he replied, *"you remembered my name."* And that was it.

The poor are often the forgotten ones. No one remembers them, let alone their names. On the day I yelled out his name, Richard couldn't believe that he had been remembered.

In the months and years that followed, I poured my life into this young man. Where I went, he came. We did life together. Today he is a pastor and is pouring his life into another one or two…and so it goes on.

Meeting Zohra

Amanda[3]

(Delhi, India)

Amanda and her husband, Dean, came to Delhi from Australia. While living there, they had their first baby, a beautiful little girl. Amanda is a teacher and Dean a town planner.

I met Zohra when friends of hers came to us and asked us to pray for her because she was very ill. After being led up a narrow, dark, dirt-encrusted staircase toward her room, we found her huddled on a simple wood and rope bed. She was little more than skin and bones, but a broad smile lit up her face when she recognised the children that had brought me to see her.

"A salaam valaekum," I said, offering a greeting of peace to this tiny, frail woman as I sat beside her. I explained I had come because I had heard she was sick, and as I sat and listened, she began to pour out her heart and share her life with me.

Zohra's family had moved into our community the year before when their slum – the biggest in Delhi and just across the river from us - had been demolished by the Government in a "clean-up" project that had left thousands homeless and pushed up rents in our neighborhood by twenty-five percent.

"Our life is hard. There are many problems," she whispered. "My husband used to be a carpenter until he lost his eye in an accident. Now he can't see well enough to do that work. He pulls a cycle-rickshaw day in day out, but still can't make enough to pay our rent of 1000 Rupees (about US $20) per month. This is the cheapest place we could find. We don't even have running water or a toilet."

Then she introduced me to her daughter Azra, who had escaped from her violent husband and returned to her parent's tiny home after he poured fuel over her and set her alight, burning a large portion of her back. Azra looked around seventeen or eighteen years old, her huge brown eyes full of fear and uncertainty.

"What hope is there for my daughter now?" Zohra whispered, since it would be impossible to find another husband for Azra now that she had been "tried and found wanting." I knew that life without a husband was unimaginable in Indian culture, since Azra would be consigned to a life of scorn and contempt in her community. She would be viewed as useless and in constant danger of abuse and rape from men if she ventured outside, or if she were left home alone.

Zohra, her broken-hearted mother, was so weak she could hardly stand, but she hadn't even mentioned her own illness yet. Zohra had advanced tuberculosis. While medicines for TB are supposed to be provided free by Government clinics, someone had lied to Zohra, telling her that the free ones wouldn't work, but that the medicines they could provide for her were "guaranteed." So Zohra was being charged 50 rupees a day by some quack in private practice making a small packet from one of the poorest people I knew. He was literally draining the life from this family!

As I listened to Zohra, my mind was whirling, seeking practical solutions, working out how I could possibly help Zohra in her desperation. Though I offered to pray with her, I felt horribly uncomfortable and inadequate. Knowing I could get Zohra onto the proper medicines for free from the nearby Government hospital, I pounced on that one practical solution and set it up. And for sometime afterwards I avoided visiting Zohra again. That frail little body, that dark little room, the tragedy of the family's situation – it was all more than I could bear.

After a few weeks Zohra called me back. "Where have you been?" she asked. "Others come and talk, but you pray - and that is the most important thing!"

What I had 'needed' was to be some kind of professional helper, someone who gets in there and does something useful - and then gets out again. But what Zohra had really longed for was a friend. Though over time I found some practical ways to help the family, whenever there were no quick solutions or complete answers, I had to remind myself that more than anything else Zohra just wanted me to visit and pray with her.

Some months later, while I was on leave in Australia, I learned that Zohra had died, and I wept for all she had suffered, for her family, for the loss of such a beautiful life. I celebrate her meeting Jesus, knowing in my deepest being that her suffering has finally ended. She was such a dignified woman, who taught me so much, and though she was the poorest woman I have ever known, through her I have become richer.

A Child Lying In The Road

Craig Greenfield

(Phnom Penh, Cambodia)

Craig Greenfield is the International Coordinator of Servants. Though he wrote this article while living in Phnom Penh, working with children orphaned by HIV/AIDS, he and his wife, Nayhouy, and their two children, Jayden and Micah, have since relocated to Vancouver, Canada, in order to begin a community working with the inner-city poor there.

Racing round the corner on my way to the meeting a little faster than usual, I thought of all the things I had to do that day. I was showing a visitor around town and I also had my own errands that needed completing. I was unsure of how I would fit it all in and the pressure was starting to make me feel flustered. I twisted the accelerator handle on our scooter and felt the bike surge under us. Not far to go, I thought to myself. We're only a couple of minutes late and we're nearly there. I'm sure they'll wait. As we slowed to negotiate a pothole, I looked up ahead and saw that there in the middle of the road lay a little boy, about eleven years old. A car had slowed to edge past him and the boy seemed oblivious - either asleep or unconscious. It was your typical Good Samaritan situation, but I was certainly not in the mood for interruptions. After all, living in Cambodia I came across this type of situation reasonably often. He was probably just a glue-sniffer - wasted and sleeping it off. I sighed, pulled over and stopped. We shook the boy and quickly realised that he was intellectually disabled and didn't seem able to speak. My friend, knowing we were late, suggested we give him some money and be on our way. But I knew that cash would not really help this boy. No one seemed to know who he was or where he had come from.

I propped him up on the front of my bike and we took off for the meeting. On reaching our destination he seemed to come alive. Someone at the meeting gave him some fruit, which he accepted with a grunt, and then proceeded to munch voraciously, most of the juice ending up on the upholstery of the office furniture. I apologised with embarrassment and tried in vain to keep him under control.

After the meeting we returned to the spot where we had found the boy and asked again if anyone knew who he was. An old man with a cigarette balanced on his bottom lip informed me with a pout that the boy was just a crazy street kid—mentally deficient and not worth the trouble I was going to. My heart sank as I realised this was a problem that wasn't going to go away.

I spent the afternoon making calls to every orphanage I could think of. None would take a mentally disabled child. It remained unspoken, but I knew they reserved their places for children who were easy to look after. In fact, in Cambodia, most orphanages are full of children who are not even orphans, merely poor. Cambodians shrewdly treat these well-meaning (often church-run) orphanages as a boarding school, where they can drop their kids off for a good education, then reap the rewards when they leave as fully educated adults. I cursed the system as I slammed down the phone after yet another rejection. I knew that particular mission orphanage was only a third full, and yet they were unwilling to take him! Why didn't they focus on the kids who really needed a place rather than the cute ones who looked good in the fundraising photos, or the lucrative babies who were easy to adopt out to rich Westerners? Finally, I found a drop-in centre for street kids that had a residential facility. The only problem was the kids were free to come and go if they wished. I knew he would run away if given half a chance as he had already tried to run away from me a couple of times. But what choice did I have? With my heart full of misgivings, I took him over to the center and the staff there welcomed him kindly. "Give me a call if there are any problems," I said as I left, feeling sure it wouldn't be long before I heard from them. Sure enough, the next day they called, saying that at first light that morning he had taken off all his clothes and run away. They apologized profusely and I told them not to worry, spending the next couple of hours driving the streets looking for him in vain.

Two weeks later a Cambodian friend called, "Craig, do you remember that boy you were with a couple of weeks ago?"

"Yes," I replied.

"Well, I think he's in front of my house — and Craig...he's not wearing any clothes!"

This time I took him home and my wife gamely agreed to put him up till we could find a more permanent place for him to live. Over the next few days, we found out that he had been living on the streets for years, surviving without language by pointing at food and throwing a head-banging tantrum if the shopkeepers didn't give it to him.

We witnessed this ritual a couple of times when he accompanied us to the market and marvelled at how he survived using this cunning method despite his difficulty with speech.

Soon we were able to arrange for him to go and live with a kind-hearted Cambodian foster family. He needed twenty-four-hour care and supervision. He couldn't go to the toilet by himself or even dress or wash himself. We didn't know his name and he couldn't speak to tell us, so the foster family decided to give him a new name. Biblically, a new name often signifies a change in circumstance or status. Saul became Paul. Abram became Abraham. And so it was with this boy, as we gave him the new name "Vundy". And with the new name came a new status for Vundy – as a beloved son, valued, cared for, and part of the family.

Within weeks, he had learnt a handful of words, was looking much healthier and had begun to settle down. My reward came every time I went to visit. Vundy would see me coming from the street and come rushing out, shouting excitedly one of the few words he had learnt: "Papa, Papa."

I look back now to the day I found Vundy lying in the middle of the road and think about what I would have missed out on had I kept to my busy agenda and 'important' timetable. I would have missed out on helping this little boy who had no-one to call "Papa."

Ricco – A Boy In Search Of His Father

Christian Schneider

(Manila, Philippines)

Christian Schneider, a nurse from Switzerland, arrived in Manila in the late 1980s, living in its slum communities for a further thirteen years. During his time in Manila, God worked through him to raise up "Onesimo," a therapeutic drug rehabilitation community for Manila's street youth.

A Mother Weeps

The air is hot and thick in the tiny house of the squatter community: corrugated iron roof, thin plywood walls, bare concrete floor and hardly any furniture. Now, during the night time, a *'panhik'* (a thin mat made from straw) covers the floor and serves as a bed for the three brothers.

Ten-year-old Ricco, the youngest boy, suddenly wakes, his body tense and his ears straining to understand what the darkness conceals. Finally his eyes adjust to the dim light of a solitary candle and the silhouette of his mother on their one wooden bench, her face covered with both hands and quietly sobbing. Ricco loves his mother more than anything else in life. The small woman – hardly taller than Ricco - is carrying far too many burdens as she struggles to raise her boys on her own. Ricco feels a stone swelling in his throat, but he mustn't cry – he has to be strong. He mustn't add any more to his mother's load. He has to be strong because his brothers are not, and his father, who he never knew, is gone.

One Day I Will Be Strong

At 5 am, his mother sneaks out of the hut to work until 10 pm that night, returning totally exhausted, unable to listen to the concerns of her three boys. Seven days a week, she puts in 17 hours labor in a dusty market in a busy city in the south of the Philippines. Day after day, she lugs heavy baskets of vegetables, dividing and sorting the produce, trying to make it attractive to the passing buyers. And after all this effort, her earnings will hardly cover food and schooling for the children, and the heaviness of it all is making her old before her time.

Ricco's thoughts turn to what happened the evening before: yet again, there was a fight among the horde of wild kids in the neighborhood. Like so many times before, his older brother was teased and laughed at, seemingly without any reason.

His brother tried to defend himself hopelessly. An older, drunken guy grabbed his arms, twisted them painfully and ordered the crowd of kids to beat him up. Those kids were like devils, hitting and kicking him senselessly, yelling and laughing crazily. Ricco stood there paralysed by anger and shame, unable to do anything about what he was witnessing. How he hated to be humiliated and powerless like this. If you can't hit back, you get crushed in this sprawling, lawless squatter area.

"One day I will be strong and I will take revenge for the pain of my mother and of my brothers." Those were his last thoughts before he finally drifted back to sleep again.

I Want to Kill My Father

By the time Ricco is thirteen years old, he has begun working in his spare time as a street vendor so that he won't be a burden to his mother like his older brothers. On the streets he makes new friends, members of the local gang. These guys are strong, and they offer him a sense of belonging and protection. With this crowd there is always something happening, something to distract from the monotony and pain of life in a slum. Tired of the humiliation in his neighborhood and weary of hearing his mother weep, Ricco begins to stay away from school and eventually from home.

More and more he feels his father is to blame for the life he is trapped in, and those feelings begin to consume him. His hatred for his father drives him with a coldblooded energy that earns him the fear and respect of his fellow gang members.

By the age of fourteen, he is the founder of his own street gang: the Red Devils. Under Ricco's leadership, the Red Devils grow fast in numbers and influence. By the time Ricco is seventeen, there are more than 200 boys and girls under his command.

They are divided into four groups in different neighborhoods, each with its own subleader, who meets weekly with Ricco. They live by stealing, hold-ups and drug deals. A few times Ricco ends up in jail, but manages to get released quickly due to the many connections he has developed. In the inter-gang battles, Ricco always fights in the frontline, dodging the petrol-bombs, knives and other home-made weapons. They fight against each other and against the living death of a life without hope for the future. All the girls in the gang are available to Ricco, but this wild rollercoaster of drugs, violence and sex never seems to take him anywhere, and never seems to satiate the deep pain and hunger within. And all the time, this furious ride is fuelled by the ever-present hatred towards his father. Ricco has become possessed by this one thought: "I want to find my father - and kill him."

Bloodlust

One day, in a confrontation with a rival gang over turf or wounded pride, Ricco is chosen to solve the conflict for the Red Devils by slugging it out with someone from the opposing gang. But as the two gangs form their battle lines behind their chosen protagonists, everything rapidly careens out of control, the atmosphere growing hot with abusive taunts and obscenities. Suddenly Ricco notices that the guy chosen to fight him is pulling a big knife from the back of his pants. Instinctively Ricco swings at him with a sawn-off pool cue, smashing him hard across the forehead. His opponent falls to the ground, but immediately drags himself up to his feet again, knife in hand. Ricco swings again, even harder, smashing the length of wood across his opponent's head for the second time.

This time the boy is badly hurt, and only just manages to struggle to his feet.

The screams of the Red Devils grow louder and even more hysterical as they sense victory. The opposing gang flees in disarray, their fallen leader badly dazed and struggling to keep up. But the Red Devils are not satisfied with this easy victory: they become like men possessed, filled with a bloodlust that knows neither mercy nor reason. They have become predators, determined to hunt down and kill their wounded prey. One of Ricco's gang reaches the struggling leader first and thrusts a knife deep into his back. Others follow, and knife after knife is driven home in a wild frenzy. Ricco, too, mindless and drunk with a thirst for blood, pushes his own knife deep into the boy, whose life is draining away, filling the gutter and staining the dirt.

On the Run

As the boy convulses and breathes his last, Ricco snaps out of his hate-driven spell and realises fully what has happened: he has killed the son of the most powerful drug lord in the city. The police he does not fear – they can always be bought off - but the family of his victim will not rest until Ricco is dead too. This is the law of revenge. Now it is Ricco's turn to run.

Ricco creeps back to the market for one last meeting with his mother. "Mum, something terrible has happened. It is all father's fault...but I love you mum..." He cries, kisses and embraces his astonished mother.

Then he takes the next bus and travels aimlessly through the country for three months, moving from one hiding place to another. From a relative he hears of a cousin living in Manila. This cousin, he learns, stays with a group called Onesimo, and has started a new life without drugs. Ricco has few choices left. He finds his cousin, and with him shelters in one of the youth training communities of Onesimo, located in an inner-city squatter settlement.

Another Life is Possible

Before being accepted into the long-term therapeutic Onesimo community, Ricco goes on a two-week admission retreat at Camp

Rock, which is located on an island, a half day trip from Manila. Though it is the most popular tourist destination near Manila, due to its natural beauty and clean beaches, most poor people from the capital have never been there. Those who come to Camp Rock get to experience nature as a life giving and beautiful gift from God rather than an arbitrary and hostile force.

At Camp Rock, the evenings are filled with singing, telling stories, reading the Bible and prayer, but Ricco still has one dominating thought: to find his father in order to kill him.

One evening, a local pastor asks the campers to close their eyes and quiet their hearts. Ricco closes his eyes. "Imagine - just for yourself - that Jesus is standing in front of you, looking directly into your eyes," Pastor Noel says. "You can't evade his gaze. His eyes are filled with love, an everlasting love, and you feel it. It is just for you. How will you answer him?" Suddenly Ricco feels a warm power flooding through his whole body, from head to toe, and he begins to weep. As Pastor Noel takes him into his arms, Ricco sobs, "I have to leave this place, please let me go." But the leaders and some of the new campers gather around Ricco and pray as Pastor Noel says: "Do not run anymore, this is your day, give Jesus a chance. He loves you, he loves you unconditionally!"

This encounter with God's power convinced Ricco that another life was possible, and he chose to enter the long-term therapeutic Onesimo community.

I Belong to God

Over time, through many months of struggle, prayer and self-doubt, as Ricco was embraced by the peers he lived with in the Onesimo community and lovingly fathered by an older leader, his hatred and thirst for revenge towards his father were transformed into a deep longing to meet him in order to forgive him and be reconciled. A few months after Rico arrived at Onesimo, a lawyer on its Board investigated the police report regarding the gang murder and found that though the names of four other gang members were listed, Ricco's name was not - and so there was no case against him.

"In our Onesimo community, Angelito and Jaymare, who are like older brothers, helped me again and again out of my many depressions," explains Ricco.

"They encouraged me repeatedly and promised that if I would not give up, if I would not back-slide, and if I would keep praying, I would find my real father. This hope, their faith, really gave me strength."

Ricco's mother, with the help of an Onesimo social worker, finally managed to track down Ricco's father in a province three hours from Manila. Onesimo workers counseled Ricco and visited his father to prepare them both for their reunion. His father organized a fiesta (party), inviting relatives and friends to welcome Ricco. As Ricco arrived at his father's house accompanied by three Onesimo staff, the lights were dimmed and the words of an emotional Tagalog song called "Anak" ("child") began to play. Then, in true Filipino fashion, fireworks were set-off.

Once everyone was quiet, Ricco climbed out of the car, stood in front of his father, and began to talk about the years of hardship faced by the family, of the shame of poverty, and the pain and desperation of growing up without his father. He talked about his hatred, his thirst for revenge, his moral decay, and his dream for a new and united family.

After a brief silence, Ricco's father haltingly asked his son for forgiveness, tears streaming down his face. After embracing his son, Ricco's father began to tell his story: how when Ricco was still a baby, they were very, very poor and he could barely feed his family; how he felt so powerless and crushed by injustice that he turned to the armed wing of the communist party, the NPA (New Peoples Army), to fight the Marcos dictatorship. In one battle he got hurt very badly, almost died, and the injuries left him partially paralysed. In such a condition he could not face going back to his family and adding another burden to his young wife and the mother of his three sons. As time passed, he lost all contact with Ricco's mother, and the thought of returning grew more and more difficult. A slight speech defect and big scars across his abdomen confirmed his story.

Ricco now attends the Onesimo School and helps his community with the rehabilitation of other street youth. His father has moved back with his mother, fulfilling his dream for a united family. Though Ricco still has to face up to some of the consequences of his past, he knows he has been given a chance at a new life, and he doesn't want to waste it. "The avenger of my old life might catch up with me and kill me," he says. "But I don't fear death anymore. Now I know where I am going and that I belong to God."

A God Of Loving Justice, Not Fear

Neil[4]

(Delhi, India)

Neil, a civil engineer from New Zealand, arrived in Delhi in the late 1990s. Neil has returned to New Zealand since the events of this story, but his love for India remains, and he visits Delhi whenever he can and continues to maintain his friendship with those mentioned in the story below.

I remember so well the confusion of sights and sounds that assailed me during my first days in Delhi - street vendors hawking their wares, vehicle horns blasting incessantly, music blaring from portable radios and televisions, people talking and arguing in the overcrowded streets, and the barking of dogs, cawing of crows and mawing of cows. I arrived during the hot season, and the heat and humidity made me feel as if I'd just stepped into a steamship boiler room. Coming from cool, green New Zealand, I felt overwhelmed by the cacophony and the swirling signs of life, but I knew that Delhi was where God had called me.

My teammates, David and Amy Jo, had arrived in Delhi ahead of me, and I found a one-bedroom 'flat' just a few doors away from them, with just enough space for a bed and table, a tiny kitchenette and a toilet area with floor space for bucket bathing. With time and patience, I began to recognize the harsh sounds of the Urdu language, and I was able to have simple conversations with my neighbors.

Everything seemed to be flowing smoothly, but then Amy Jo became very ill during the final months of her first pregnancy. Over the course of only a few days, she fell into coma due to a rapidly growing brain tumour and was hospitalized for emergency brain surgery and a simultaneous caesarean to save her baby. Amy Jo regained consciousness long enough to glimpse her newborn daughter before slipping back into coma and dying. Distraught, David left soon after to return to the States with little Kiran. After only a few short months in this new city, I felt devastated and very alone in my adopted neighborhood without the help of my two good friends.

A few days after David and Kiran's departure, I was returning home from language school when I was hailed by a young man who had just moved into a room across the alley from me. He greeted me with an enthusiastic, "Hello sir!" But it soon became obvious that his English vocabulary did not include much more than that. Fortunately, his younger brother (who was studying English) saw the difficulty we were having and came to our rescue. The young man's name was Om Prakash, though everybody referred to him as O.P., and his younger brother's name was Sunil. They lived together in one room with their little sister, Neetu. Their parents were in a rural village two hours away by train, and the kids had been sent to Delhi in order to get a better education. My friendship with O.P. Neetu, and particularly Sunil grew steadily. Before long, they introduced me to their parents, and I felt as though I had been accepted as part of their family, which was a great comfort during this dark and lonely time.

I spent many afternoons after language school playing simple board games (especially ludo!) with my three friends, and we began to share more deeply with each other. They practiced their English with me, and in turn helped me get my tongue around more of the local language. This proved to be a wonderful adjunct to my language school curriculum. At school I was instructed in pure, 'correct' Urdu, but here in the neighborhood my friends taught me the informal and colloquial slang that the locals really used with each other. Sunil, in particular, seemed fascinated with trying to understand my reasons for coming to India and peppered me with questions about my life. As our relationship and trust in each other deepened, I began to share more and more with him about my faith in Jesus, while he reciprocated by explaining his belief in the Hindu gods. We were learning from one another, helping one another to understand each other's culture, hopes and fears. A day came when I explained that the God I knew was a God of love, and Sunil was astounded. He found it difficult to grasp. Searching for the right words, he explained to me that the gods he worshipped engendered fear, and that for most people he knew, worship was based on a sense of duty and a fear of the consequences if they failed to offer the right sacrifices. Over a period of weeks and months I shared with Sunil and his family more about Jesus and about God's love for each and every one of us.

The more Sunil came to trust me as a true friend, the more and more he wanted to know about my friend, Jesus. I invited him to attend church with me one Sunday morning, and he remained quiet and thoughtful throughout the meeting, commenting later about how different it was from his visits to the local Hindu temple. After that our discussions deepened even further, and he continued to accompany me to church and to the youth group meetings, which I helped to lead.

When Sunil became very ill with typhoid fever, I prayed for him and helped get him good medical treatment, much to his family's relief.

During our discussions I began to share with him about how I had become a follower of Jesus, and how Jesus could free us from the devastating effects of sin and selfishness in our own lives and in the world around us. Sunil could see how the things the Bible describes as 'sin' were crippling his own life and the lives of so many others in India, and his questions began to flow more rapidly.

When I had to return home to New Zealand for a period of seven months, Sunil and I continued to keep in touch. Just prior to my return to India, I was thrilled to receive an email from Sunil saying that he wanted to follow Jesus and to leave behind the many other Hindu gods he had worshipped for so long. He had weighed up the cost that this decision would have for his life and decided that following Jesus would be worth the price he might have to pay. On my return, we met and Sunil prayed that Jesus would become Lord of his whole life. After so many months of searching, wrestling, and struggling, Sunil was immediately filled with an overpowering joy that he could barely contain, and he was desperate to tell the rest of his family about his decision as soon as he could. Despite my fears, they accepted his decision and wanted to know more - with the exception of Sunil's older sister, who lived a short distance from our neighborhood. Though she had also become my friend, she tried to convince Sunil to go back to worshipping Hindu gods. He steadfastly resisted, and over time she came to accept Sunil's decision and respect him for his courage and conviction. As Sunil and I shared the gospel with his family, one by one they came to accept Jesus as their Lord. Sunil's mother had become such a radiant and joyful person since she asked Christ into her life that her neighbors and friends often asked her why she looked so happy - and she gladly told them about her new faith and the changes it brought about in her life.

Over the past few years, as Sunil has continued to let Christ shape his life, his love for the least in his community has continued to grow. Though the great Mahatma Gandhi, who is still widely revered in India, begged his fellow Indians to forsake the caste system and consider all others as brothers, many from the upper castes still treat the poor with contempt and untouchables as subhuman. But after encountering Jesus, Sunil no longer shared this indifference towards those who were suffering or impoverished. The caste system became an anathema to him, and he began to reach out to neighbors from lower castes with love and compassion.

There are so many others like Sunil and his family who are longing to hear the good news of Jesus and his Kingdom. On this great continent - where one out of every five human beings live; where a child is born every two seconds (and of those that survive, half will be malnourished); where 88 million poor live in desperate slums; and where there are more un-reached people groups than in any other place – we must beg God to raise up workers for the harvest. And we must be ready to go and be the answer to that prayer.

You Are Family

Miriam Hadcocks

(Phnom Penh, Cambodia)

Miriam is a community worker and activist from the United Kingdom. In 2004 she spent a month in Cambodia as an intern, living with a large extended 'family' in an urban slum. This household is headed up by a big hearted matriarch named Ming (aunty) Houen, and filled with widows and orphans she has taken under her wing. Suntay is one of those orphans.

The sky above us was probably starless and cloudy, but it was impossible to tell with this worn plastic tarpaulin canopy as my ceiling. This layer of grubby plastic lowered the sky and trapped the oppressive heat, as if air was something precious that wouldn't return until the morning.

The lights were out, another power cut. And as I thought about flying out tomorrow, it struck me that in the darkness, from above, all these slums without power would appear just as they did on the maps – non-existent. Ming Houen, my landlady, brought a candle up from below, pulled over an old chair, allowed the wax to drip

66

on to the seat and pressed the bent stick into something like an upright position before retreating back downstairs. On the far side of the city, across a wide gulf of billowing tarpaulin, plastic, tin and corrugated iron, the rich people went about in well-lit streets that shone like those in heaven. But here, on the balcony of this house full of orphans, eccentric old men and tireless, wise young women that for the last four weeks I had called 'my family', Ming Houen's light was the brightest. One small candle pushing back the darkness.

It shone off the underside of the roof canopy, holding in something more beautiful than the song of the insects, which filled me with a sense of excitement and the exotic, just as it had the first night of my arrival. It was as if they sang to me mysterious nocturnal ballads of this strange land, its history, its life, its energy. As long as I could hear them, I was here, and it was real.

How strange that this image that summed up for me so much about life in Cambodia should appear only in the darkness - that the light of a city could be obscured by the light of a candle. Now as I lay in the semi-darkness, thinking back over the past month of intense heat, I was intoxicated by the grace and pain of this contradictory place.

In the street below, I could make out the scurrying of tiny malnourished, flea ridden dogs as they chased and killed huge malnourished, flea ridden rats. In the lower floor of the house opposite, lit, no doubt, by an equally upright light, a group of young men chatted and laughed in an easy, friendly language that I failed to understand but whose meaning was clear, universal. And here, on a balcony that jutted between the street below and the sky above, between the last four weeks and the rest of my life, between two entirely alien cultures, between two foreigners, stood my housemate, Suntay, and me.

We had nothing in common. Nothing at all. Which, in itself, seemed odd, considering how much I had come to love her.

Admittedly, I had spent the last decade of my life in the lower echelons of the British economic structure, and I knew what it was to sit in the dole office or the Citizen's Advice and cry because that was the easiest way to get the money that would feed you for the next week. But I had no idea what it was to watch your younger brothers go hungry. I didn't know what it was, aged six, eight, ten, to get up and travel miles to sell what little you had so that not only you, but your family, could eat that evening. I knew what it was to live in a van (on occasions, with three other people), and to be disdained for doing so, or in the cheapest little room you could find, and to still pay more than you could afford. But I had no idea what it was to curl up on the ground, after your hard day of walking and bartering, not just for pennies, but for your whole existence, surrounded by ash and rubble, all that remained after your slum had been burned down. But Suntay did.

And I knew what it was to gain an education. To work for it, to see it as your purpose. To go further in these endeavors than any previous generation of your family. I knew what it was to struggle with exams, and to work in menial jobs to pay your way through school. But I had no idea what it was like, aged twenty, to go to several hours of school, endless hours of work, and then, because you have the good fortune to temporarily share a house with your teacher, to ask and ask and ask (but never beg) for more hours of education. To go over and over and over minor details of pronunciation, to ignore the ridicule of those in other rooms to whom the difference between a "J" and a "G" seemed unimportant, when you knew exactly how much could one day depend on it. But she did, and perhaps there had been something in our mutual struggles – her with the consonants of English, me with the vowels of Khmer, that had unified us. And here we stood, breaking the quiet darkness with our laughter, echoing the young men opposite and the young girls listening in the house behind us, as she took her last opportunity to teach me long sentences in Khmer and then not tell me what they meant, as we exchanged the mutual language of "goodbye... I love you... I will miss you...", getting ready for the dawn that would be much darker than the present night.

I knew what it was to lose a parent, and to grieve, and to struggle with all the complex emotions of such a relationship. But it was

Suntay who knew what it was to grow up in an orphanage, not because her parents were dead, but because they were unable to afford the upkeep of her and her brothers. And what could it have been, in those circumstances, whilst still a child herself, to take on the role of parent, working and caring for her young family, as she watched first one, and then another, parent die of AIDS - an eventuality which, had she been born in my shoes, could have been so easily avoided. But both of us knew what it was to find a welcome in the finely balanced chaos of this home full of hard-working, soft-laughing youth, whose inner hope shone as brightly as the gentle candle light against the encroaching darkness.

And then, as suddenly as the cockerels would start crowing in a few hours, she stopped laughing. She smiled her smile that spoke more of sadness than happiness, rolled her eyes, and paused.

"You are family," she said. "You understand?"

"Yes," I replied. "I understand."

"No," she insisted. "You are family. You understand?"

"Yes I understand," I said, perhaps a little put out. "So are you." And again she laughed, but this time without humor.

"Ah, sister," she said – for the first time, not 'teacher' – "you are family."

How could I possibly know what she meant? How could I begin to presume what such a precious word meant to her? But I knew the value of it, because I knew the value of what this family had come to mean to me over these four weeks.

The next morning, sometime around 6.00, Houen, Suntay and I said a hasty goodbye as the heat, predictably, returned. My sister and I walked together through the streets, already full of sunlight and people, whom I greeted and farewelled for the last time. The familiar Phnom Penh fragrance – a heady mixture of traffic fumes, decaying vegetables, hot, damp earth and pungent incense, which had become as sweet, rich and welcome as the place it filled – was completed by the aroma of cooking breakfasts. The people consuming them were, as ever, lively, welcoming and inquisitive. Along with Sunday afternoons, this was always my favorite time to walk through the slum – and over the month, the

69

stares and friendly prods had given way to a ritual of games with the children, exchanges of bows and handshakes, recitations of "hello, how are you? I am fine," and in return, "Sursday, sok sa bai dtei? Sok sa bai." Often this would lead to equally meaningful yet incomprehensible exchanges with their parents, both of us pointing at the contents of various bowls and plates and them laughing as I tried to repeat what they named. It always amused me that no matter how often I was told what something was called, I still had no idea as to its actual identity. The general amusement seemed to be mutual.

But no time for these lessons today. Slipping through the gap between the buildings and leaving the slum – which immediately became invisible – for the last time, we reached the road. Here my sister called me a motorbike taxi and engaged, on my behalf, in long and complicated directions. I turned to give the driver my bag, and she was gone.

Yet six months later, she is still very much with me here in England, as if she vanished not into the streets behind me, but into my consciousness. Certainly, there are moments and memories from Cambodia that still make me weep, either with joy or sadness, anger or delight, but it is Suntay, that evening on the balcony, that takes me back there. And maybe that is the one thing we have in common, that in one sense or the other, chances are, neither one of us will ever leave.

Knowing Names, Affirming Dreams:
Concluding Reflections On Community

Kristin Jack

We ask ourselves, who am I to be brilliant, gorgeous, talented and famous? Actually, who are you not to be? You are a child of God. Your playing small doesn't serve the world. There's nothing enlightened about shrinking so that other people won't feel insecure around you. We are all meant to shine, as children do. We are born to make manifest the glory of God that is with us. It's not just in some of us, it's in everyone. And as we let our own light shine, we unconsciously give other people permission to do the same. As we are liberated from our own fear, our presence automatically liberates others.

Marianne Williamson[5]

Taller and skinnier than his six siblings, with a dazzling grin, gentle friendliness and probing curiosity, Phanna was a boy whose searching eyes always seemed to be full of hope, and his heart full of dreams. Everybody liked Phanna.

Susan and I got to know Phanna two months after we arrived in Cambodia in 1994. Full of energy and youthful idealism, we had chosen to live in a riverside slum community known as *Chrang Bak*, or 'broken riverbank,' where we rented a tiny, one-room bamboo shack. After learning that there was a Bible study group meeting in the small home of a couple very close by, we joined them, eager to make new friends and improve our language skills.

One evening, Vee, the group leader's wife, came to our door and nervously explained that there was a man in a house nearby who was probably dying. Though he wasn't part of our Bible study group, she felt God had spoken to her – "like an electric shock" - and said that the group should go and pray for him and offer whatever help we could. She wanted to know if we would come too?

Like Vee, we felt nervous – our language was still very limited, and we didn't know this family at all – but we agreed. We arrived

71

to find that six or seven of the group were already crowded inside, all neighbors who lived nearby. In the dimly candle-lit room, Phanna's father was lying just inside the door, clearly not too many days away from death. Sue and I squeezed in beside his bed and clasped our hands together in the traditional prayer-like Cambodian greeting, and he, with much effort, greeted us back with a feeble whisper. From the look of his emaciated body and sunken eyes, we guessed that he was dying of cancer. The members of the Bible study group gathered around and prayed for Phanna's dad. Then, one by one, they offered him words of encouragement and hope, offering testimonies about how God had made himself real to them and how they had come to experience forgiveness and new life. Over the next two weeks the members of the group continued to visit and pray, helping with nursing cares, washing and feeding.

Within the month, Phanna's dad died, but the day before he slipped from consciousness, his eyes widened and he sat up in bed and called his wife and children to gather around him. With great effort he pointed at the spirit-altar that adorns most Cambodian homes and asked them to take it down. Turning to face his wife and children, he begged them to stop offering sacrifices to the spirits and to begin following Jesus instead.

Over the next few months we developed a deep friendship with Phanna's mother, Channy. She had a penetrating mind, and she probed us with searching questions about the Christian life, which was so different from the Buddhist faith she had grown up with. She started to become a key figure in the neighborhood Bible study group, and her relationship with Jesus became more and more vital. Her bubbly nature and lively sense of humor made her a great ambassador for her new faith, and there were very few of the neighbors who didn't get to hear the story of how Jesus could change your life! Susan and I helped the group start an income generating project recycling waste paper into stationary products, and Channy quickly emerged as one of the group's natural leaders.

Throughout 1994 and 1995, the eight families involved in the paper making group– all dirt poor—were making good money for the first time in their lives.

Moreover, many of our neighbors were coming to faith, and the Bible study group had grown quite large. About this time, another man in the slum, whose marriage was breaking up, fell in love with Channy, and they moved in together despite our best efforts to persuade them otherwise. By late 1996 Channy was pregnant, and in mid-1997, she gave birth to a beautiful daughter named Saraah. Later that year, three years after her first husband's death, Channy began to lose weight, feel weak, have recurring bouts of diarrhea, and develop a nagging cough. Then an abscess formed on her neck and wouldn't heal, even after Susan put her on a course of high-powered antibiotics. After many delays Channy was admitted for tests and diagnosed with tuberculosis, but even worse, her blood results had come back from the hospital marked "HIV positive."

As we stared at the piece of paper announcing Channy's test results, tears rolling down our faces, we felt stupid for not figuring out what her husband had died of three years earlier. Though AIDS had been no more than a rumour in Cambodia in 1994, and neither Susan nor I had ever seen a case up until then, the disease had since become rampant, with 180,000 Cambodians rapidly infected and dying.

For the next six agonising months, as we provided 24-hour on-call nursing care for Channy, she grew more and more consumed by tuberculosis and the other opportunistic infections that invaded her body, reducing it to a barely recognisable skeleton. On the day Channy died, Phanna - who had been nine when his father died and twelve when he lost his mother - fell to his knees beside her body and wept.

Saraah, with good medical support, made it through to three-and-a-half before her body finally gave up and she was buried in a shallow grave near their house. Susan and I continued to try and keep an eye on the kids and help them as they grew. In particular we hoped and prayed for Phanna to fulfil his potential.

By fifteen, he had left school, desperate to try and bring in some income to help feed his younger siblings, even though their step-father, to his credit, stuck by the six step-children, supporting and caring for them, whereas many other Cambodian men had cut and run in similar situations. We managed to find Phanna an apprenticeship with a Christian group that taught welding and metal work skills, where he would have an opportunity to make a good income from the high quality metal goods this group was producing and selling.

But after about eighteen months, Phanna became unsettled and eventually dropped out, instead taking up odd jobs around Chrang Bak and further afield – at one time collecting garbage for recycling; at another carrying two heavy pots on a bamboo pole across his shoulders to cook and sell noodles to hungry passers-by for a few cents. The group that had agreed to teach him metal-work skills were annoyed with Phanna and with us, and we were embarrassed - but we were determined not to give up on him. We remembered that he had earlier expressed an interest in learning computer skills, so Susan went door to door, from computer business to computer business, till she eventually found one that was prepared to take Phanna on as an apprentice. At first Phanna was enthusiastic and faithful in his attendance, but eventually this resolve faded and soon he was more often absent than present.

Twice now we'd made a big effort for Phanna, and twice he'd let us down. Life in Cambodia is tenuous and hard, the poverty extreme. Didn't he understand that opportunities like these only come around once in a lifetime?

We heard rumours from some of our other neighbors that Phanna wasn't doing well, and that he had been seen a few times down at one of the local gambling hangouts, a cock-fighting pit. A few weeks later, during the rainy season, I bumped into Phanna as he was taxiing people home across the village floodwater in a borrowed wooden canoe to earn some extra money. Phanna was his usual, smiling self, and it was hard not to be won over by that beautiful grin.

My anger dissipating, I asked, "Phanna, what's your dream for your life?"

Phanna's grin grew wider and his eyes rolled up, as if searching the heavens for his answer. "Puu (Uncle), what I really want to be is a translator for a missionary, so I can help tell people about Jesus."

Startled, I blinked a few times. "But Phanna, you hardly speak any English at all. And there are not that many missionaries in Chrang Bak, apart from Susan and I, and we don't need a translator. Can't you think of something more practical and realistic so you can help look after your family?"

Phanna shrugged his shoulders. "Puu, you asked me what my dream was, and that's it."

After that we didn't see Phanna for a few months, so we guessed he had wandered off in search of more odd jobs somewhere further afield. But the next time I bumped into him, his grin seemed bigger than ever.

"Puu, I have a great new job!" he told me. "I'm working for Pastor Keros from the Philippines. Have you met him yet? I'm his translator!"

We had seen this Filipino family move into our area a few months before, and we knew they'd started teaching English classes and Sunday school. But we didn't know that they'd employed Phanna as their translator, nor that Phanna had made quantum-leap progress with his English studies as he translated Pastor Keros' preaching.

Now, three years later, Phanna has completed three years of Bible college, scooping up the prize for 'best preacher' along the way, and in his free time, he has begun reaching out to street kids in our area, most of whom are using yama (amphetamines) and sniffing glue. More recently he joined the TASK team, teaching life-skills to young people who are working their way off drugs. Phanna teaches the Scriptures, strums a guitar, and plays football with them. If they want, he cuts their hair, hugs them when they're crashing, shares his story, and listens to theirs. But mostly his goal is to remind them that there is a God who loves them. For even when your start in life has been full of pain, confusion and loss, Phanna knows there is a God who redeems us and who can redeem our dreams. Not one single street-kid, no matter how messed up, is beyond the reach of God's love as far as Phanna is concerned.

Every so often, Phanna drops around so that I can study the Bible in Khmer with him, and he can let off steam about the pressures and frustrations of his ministry. From Phanna we have learnt that the seeds of some dreams are birthed in the midst of great pain, and that if your dream is the same as God's dream, nothing can stand in its way. We have also learnt that everyone should be given the chance to pursue their dreams, because there is nothing as empowering as seeing your dream come true. Today, Phanna's dream is to become a missionary, a messenger and courier of God's love—and he is living his dream.

As you have read through the stories in this section on Community, we hope you have come to see that we all - no matter how poor or rich - need someone who bothers to remember our names, a friend who will listen to and seek to understand us, someone with whom we can share our struggles and triumphs, no matter how great or small those might be. While we certainly need specialists and professional development experts who work at the macro or policy level to fight against the structures that keep the poor poor, what people really long for is to be part of a community, a network of friendships in which everyone has something to contribute and where neighbors help each other out when the need arises.

1. Gutierrez is arguably South America's best known liberation theologian. This school of theology is determined to do theology from beneath: that is, to read the Bible and history from the perspective of the poor and oppressed, believing that that was the perspective of Jesus himself. Gutierrez has written prolifically, including A Theology of Liberation (Orbis, 1971/88) and We drink from our own wells (Orbis, 1984/2003).
2. Michael Duncan, quoted in Servants Among the Poor (Jenni Craig, OMF, 1998),134.
3. For security reasons, we use only first names or pseudonyms for people in India.
4. For security reasons, we use only first names or pseudonyms for people in India.
5. Marianne Williamson, Return to Love (Harper-Collins, 1994), p 190-191.

You Knew My Name
(Revelation 2:17)

Kristin Jack

you knew my name
when it was a mystery to me
you called me by name
the one I had lost
you loved my name
though I had despised it so long
you drew out my name
the one caught in my throat
and taught me the sound
of each melodic chord.
You sang my name
over and over the lies of the night
till I knew it was true.

You cried out my name
till I wept at the beauty
revealed in your pain.
You guard my name
in a sacred place
so buried in love
so deep in grace
it will last forever
never mis-said, never mis-placed
you promise to know it and say it
till I learn to sing it with you
and our voices merge
into one song (not two),
one voice, one name.
Just one. just One.
    Just One

Three

WHOLISM

Comprehensive mission springs from comprehensive salvation. Salvation is wholeness. Salvation is total humanisation. Salvation is eternal life, life in the Kingdom, life that begins here and now and touches every aspect of man's being.

Rene Padilla[1]

The glory of God is a human being fully alive.

Ireneus of Lyon[2]

INTRODUCTION: A HUMAN BEING FULLY ALIVE!

Kristin Jack

He is the image of the invisible God, the firstborn over all creation. For by him all things were created: things in heaven and on earth, visible and invisible, whether thrones or powers or rulers or authorities; all things were created by him and for him. He is before all things, and in him all things hold together. And he is the head of the body, the church; he is the beginning and the firstborn from among the dead, so that in everything he might have the supremacy. For God was pleased to have all his fullness dwell in him, and through him to reconcile to himself all things, whether things on earth or things in heaven, by making peace through his blood, shed on the cross.

(Colossians 1:15-20)

As Paul's beautiful hymn declares, we serve a savior who is working 'to redeem all things' and to restore wholeness of life to every human being—rich or poor, male or female, of every tribe and tongue. In serving this savior—who made 'peace through his blood, shed on the cross'—we, too, need to be willing to lay down our lives for others[3]: the stranger as well as the good neighbor, the enemy as well as the friend.[4] So when we see someone lying beaten and bloodied on the road to Jericho, Jesus makes it clear that we *must* stop to bandage their wounds and drag them to safety.[5] But what does this look like?

Our commitment to wholism within Servants reflects our trust in the power of that good news not only to "save" and transform individuals, but also to transform whole societal structures. We are also wary of sharp dichotomies that divide people into soul and body, or advise Christians to concentrate only on what is 'spiritual' to the exclusion of that which is 'material.' At the end of the Old Testament book of Zechariah, there is a promise of the day when God's reign in this world will be so complete that we will no longer be able to make these arbitrary distinctions between the miraculous and the mundane, the spiritual and the earthy. One day even the cooking pots will be regarded as holy![6] A day is coming when God's will shall be done on earth just as it is in heaven, and God's Kingdom will come fully upon this earth.[7]

In the meantime, Jesus calls us to seek first God's Kingdom, helping to make it a reality in our lives and in the lives of those around us—especially in the lives of the hurting, the poor, the vulnerable and the lost.

My wife, Susan, has spent the last decade working with her teammates in Servants[8] and TASK to save the lives of hundreds of malnourished children here in Cambodia.[9] At first, in the lives of these children, 'dragging the stranger to safety' meant operating a clinic where mothers could bring their children for examinations and receive vitamins, minerals, medicines and supplements. Later, it meant educating mothers and whole communities about the best way to feed and nourish healthy children on small incomes. Now, it also means leading a group that lobbies the Cambodian Ministry of Health to implement good policies on child nutrition nationwide and has pressured the Government to ban advertisements that promote infant formulas or milk powder as better than breast-feeding. By lobbying the Government until they adopted protocols and laws that would guarantee these things, Susan and others have sought to change structures, thus making the road to Jericho 'safer,' and reduce the suffering experienced by so many individuals.

And so we grapple with poverty, hunger and disease, work for justice, and lift all things to God in prayer, trusting in His grace, because we want to see the good news of Jesus proclaimed throughout the world in word, deed and power. We hope that this section on Wholism will flesh out these abstract theological principles with concrete pictures of ordinary people seeking to live out Jesus' call to love others.

Here, you will read a story about a couple who moved to India, forsaking the lives of luxury they could have led in Australia, relocating to where they felt the needs were greater and their presence would have more impact. By choosing to advocate for those in poverty and without status, they helped 750 evicted families in their neighborhood gain land rights, water, and electricity. Moreover, through their hard work, local Government policy has been changed and a pamphlet outlining people's rights has been written and published. They are now multiplying their impact even more by offering internship courses for middle-class Indian Christians, together learning what it means to live and minister among Delhi's urban poor.

You will also read about activists who put their lives on the line for one terrified Sikh family as a baying mob threatened to torch them. And you will read numerous other stories that shed light on the reality that God's love is never passive. Jesus was an activist, and his activism took him on a collision course with the powers and principalities of his day, eventually leading him to the cross.

In the face of so much suffering, a passion for justice burns within us. Yet, in our pursuit of justice, we reject the use of violence, coercion or manipulation. Instead we are prepared to embrace sacrifice and suffering in order to share in the life of Jesus and in the lives of those we have come to love. Martin Luther King, echoing Gandhi, once said that there are causes he would die for, but none he would kill for. The weapons of our warfare are not Stealth fighter planes or Molotov cocktails, but love, hope, faith, prayer, action, courage and conviction.[10] Seeking first the Kingdom of God and all its justice and righteousness[11] *will* bring us into confrontation with powers and principalities, and that will mean being prepared to lay down our lives for others. The call to fight for justice (Matthew 5:6) and the call to be active peacemakers (Matthew 5:9) are parts of the gospel that have been either forgotten or ignored by far too much of the church for far too long. But these are the ways of Jesus, and they must become our way too.[12]

Even after his ascension, and after sending his Spirit on the day of Pentecost, Jesus still seeks to be incarnate and touch this world and all its pain. But now he wants to do it through you and me. We are his body. We are his hands and feet. With the help of the Holy Spirit, God beckons us to make a conscious choice to follow Christ, and through his power to confront the violence, pain, abuse and sin of this world, wherever that may lead us.

Fighting For Land Rights Of Slum Residents

Reuben and Kim[13]

(Delhi, India)

Reuben, a lawyer, and Kim, a math and computer science honors graduate, moved from Australia into the slums of Delhi in 1995, where they continue to live, along with their two young sons, Henry and Bill.

The centre of Delhi is dominated by the capital's showpiece Government buildings, surrounded by tree-lined boulevards and lovingly kept reflective pools. But beyond this architecturally designed oasis of greenery and exquisitely crafted stone, Delhi's 15 million plus population live in one of the worlds most crowded cities, with a population density of 29,000 people per square mile. Inward migration from the surrounding states, combined with its booming birth rate, mean that Delhi is likely to be the world's third largest city by 2015.

India's much trumpeted economic growth over the last decade has created a swelling middle-class, and the urban elites continue to grow richer. But beyond the new condominiums and shopping malls, more than 3 million Delhians reside in some 1,500 shantytowns with garbage bag plastic roofs and walls. Many live in 'tents' constructed from scavenged cardboard and paper, and on average one water pump serves 1,000 residents. Yet even these are better off than the thousands who simply live on the streets, covered by nothing more than an old sari each night.

One such shantytown in Delhi is *Barapullah*. *Barapullah* was built along the bank of a fetid drainage canal located on Government land more than twenty years ago, when just a few families squatted there, but over time it became home to about 900 families, or roughly 6,000 people.

My wife and first son lived there in a little hut for 18 months in 1999-2000. Even after we moved out, we continued to visit our friends there often. On one of these visits, a friend pointed out a notice pasted onto the wall of the toilet block announcing that the Delhi City Council would in six days 'rehabilitate' residents to a relocation area twenty-five kilometers away.

A group of lawyers that some of the slum residents knew made an urgent application to the High Court, which succeeded in delaying the planned relocation for one week. However, the lawyers then informed the residents that they wanted another 50,000 rupees (about US $1,200) in order to take the case any further—a sum well out of the reach of the residents. Racking our brains over what to do next, about twenty-five residents and I decided to approach another group of NGO lawyers. Thankfully, they gave us a good hearing and offered to take this case for free.

We then held a number of community-wide meetings in the slum to inform residents of their options. After some debate, the residents decided to work in partnership with this NGO and agreed on three main things that they wanted to get out of the process: 1) a stay of four months to get the residents through winter, their children through their end of school exams, and also provide enough time for the community to gather together the fee of 7,000 rupees (US $150) that the Government was demanding from each resident to purchase a small parcel of land in the relocation area; 2) the issuing of Legal Title to their new land before they were relocated, since other relocations had promised residents land but not given them title to that land until several months after their homes had been demolished; 3) land to be made available for people who had arrived in the slum after 1998 (the council rules stated that land would only be for families who been resident in the slum since before 1998).

In court, while the NGO lawyers did a good job of representing the residents, they did not consult much with the community before the hearings, nor spend time after each hearing to explain what had happened during the proceedings, which were in English. Therefore, I tried to listen to the people and communicate their needs with the lawyers before the hearings, and then explain to the community what had been said in the hearings, translating from English back to Hindi.

When the judge asked how many residents lived in Barapullah - information the Delhi city council had but had refused to make publicly available - we embarked on the enormous task of identifying every family in the slum. We asked Kallu, one of the residents I'd gotten to know during the hearings, to lead the effort in collecting the demographic information we needed, which volunteers then brought to our house to enter into our laptop. It took several weeks of hard work, but eventually we had almost every family's name, ration card number, house number and entitlement. We then gained permission to check our list against the council's to make sure nobody had been left out, bringing discrepancies to the attention of the council, thus securing land rights for perhaps half a dozen families who would have gone landless.

In the hearings, we were shattered when the judge decided that the relocation should begin almost immediately, on the rationale that winter hadn't begun yet, even though temperatures were already down to 5 degrees celsius overnight.

Moreover, the planned relocation would take place during Eid, the biggest Muslim festival of the year—a time when families should be secure in their homes, celebrating, just as we might celebrate Christmas Day back in Australia.

As a last resort, we decided to try to negotiate directly with the Delhi City Council, which carried risks for my visa status and for Servants, but my director gave me the OK—so long as I tried to avoid controversy! Somehow, with only hours to spare before the demolition was due to begin, I managed to get through on the phone to the head of the city council department overseeing the relocation (always a minor miracle in India). After a little thought, he agreed to hold off on the relocation till after Eid. Feeling encouraged, I also suggested that it would be good to have a brochure in Hindi to give to people about to be relocated, explaining the steps they needed to take to be allocated alternative land. He agreed as well—and asked me to write it!

Meanwhile, the constant stream of people coming to Kallu's door took its toll, and one night, he came to me in tears, explaining that his family couldn't take the pressure anymore, particularly when disgruntled residents abused him if their claim didn't succeed, saying that he was 'on the take,' or that he'd actually instigated the whole relocation. People were actually beginning to make similar accusations about our family, too.

And to be honest, Kim and I were sick of the late nights, endless requests and intense stress, especially with our new baby, Bill, born just three weeks after the whole mess began. So during another community meeting, we told people that we'd tried our best, apologized for the failures, and said that Kallu's door and mine door were now shut. If people had any more complaints, they should take them directly to the lawyers. Kallu and I both felt wounded by what had happened, and through that pain, I began to share with him my trust in a God who knows what's really going on - in spite of gossip and accusations - and the example of Jesus, who was so unfairly accused.

On the morning of my next scheduled meeting with the head of the city council, where we were going to be sorting out the procedure for dealing with outstanding claims, I was shocked to see hundreds of police in riot gear near the slum. With my heart pounding, I approached the head of the police, who confirmed that they were going to forcibly remove the people today, pre-empting that afternoon's negotiation.

I borrowed a friend's mobile and phoned every contact I had in the city council, reminding them that their boss had ordered a stay on the demolition until after our meeting. As I stood there, cajoling and urging council members, watching residents calmly dismantling their houses, the police began to melt away.

Eventually, on a cold and drizzly day, after receiving title certificates, the residents of Barapullah dismantled their tiny houses brick by brick, stacking all their things onto the trucks provided by the council, and were taken to the relocation area. Of the 900 families who had lived in the slum, about 750 received land and left their former homes peacefully.

But in the relocation area, there was no running drinking water, no electricity, few buses, and when it rained, the whole area filled up like a muddy lake. After about a dozen trips to court, drinking water now comes by truck daily, most blocks now have electricity, and some of the land has been filled. One of our Indian friend's NGO began a micro-credit program in the relocation area to provide loans for people to establish small businesses, since many of them had been moved away from their source of work.

The brochure that I wrote for future relocations slowly found its way through the bureaucracy, and some of the changes I advocated, such as making the council's list of residents publicly available, were implemented in subsequent relocations. Kallu, partly as a result of this whole experience, has come to a genuine and lovely faith.

Barapullah was eventually bulldozed in April 2000 and has since been turned into a road, which is seldom used.

Finding Joy In The City Of Joy

Julius and Sara[14]

(Kolkata, India)

Julius, a carpenter and entrepreneur, and Sara arrived in Kolkata in 2001. They moved from Switzerland, a land of sumptuous lakes and mountains, to plunge themselves into the teeming poverty of India's second largest city.

Calcutta. Kolkata. Beautiful, majestic, sweeping Kolkata. Breathtaking, imperious, regal Kolkata. The goddess Kali's Hindu Kolkata. The Mogul's Muslim Kolkata. The genteel British Kolkata. Grubby, crumbling, decaying Kolkata. Corrupt, filthy, death dealing Kolkata. The living Kolkata. The dying Kolkata.

There are many Kolkatas.

Portrayed with aching beauty before the eyes of the world by Dominique Lappierre's *The City of Joy*, and laid before the conscience of the world by Mother Teresa's ministry, Kolkata is not a city you may ignore. Spend some time there. Wander along its wide boulevards shadowed on each side by graceful, crumbling Victorian architecture; let your mind's eye peel back the layers of grime and decades of neglect and see the beauty within. Spend some time in its *bustis* and slums, befriending some of the millions who struggle under centuries of fatalism, caste-ism, poverty and oppression, and see the beauty of God's sons and daughters waiting to be released. Listen, and you will hear the cry of the poor. Wait, and you will hear the call of God. Be careful. Your heart will be captured, and you will not leave easily. Something in you will have been changed.

Proud, aching Kolkata. Asia's foremost city, the artistic and cultural capital of the region. Over the previous two hundred years, she has given birth to philosophers, poets, story tellers, writers, musicians, and sages of unsurpassed genius. Blessed, yet cursed, Kolkata lies in a mineral rich corner of India under siege from alternative cycles of flood and drought, devastating earthquakes and vicious religious-political wars. And each catastrophe drives another wave of peasant farmers off their land and into this city of last hopes, where the sea of poverty grows always larger.

Beautiful, desperate Kolkata, still under the guardianship of Kali, the goddess of death—her eyes alive with terror, a garland of snakes and skulls around her neck. A city of 13 or 16 million souls (depending on whose figures you believe), with at least 6 million of those thrown into vast slums, and another half a million barely subsisting by living on the streets. A city which swells by another several million each day as hawkers and workers swarm in from the countryside in search of daily sustenance. *Is it Kali that casts this shadow of hopelessness and fatalism over the great city, condemning its poor to a life of despair?*

Away from the wide central boulevards, in the narrow back alleys and crowded ghettoes, joy sometimes gives way to fear, just as tangibly as that acrid cooking-fire smoke that blankets each slum. *So many gods to appease, so many rituals to keep.* These deities are demanding and damning, extracting a fearful price from careless worshippers. *Your poverty and pain are deserved,* they whisper. *They are the penalty for your misdeeds in previous lives.* Thus many have abandoned all hope of finding a better way, resigning themselves to their fate. *"We were born poor, we will die poor."* Perhaps the next life, the next station on this endless cycle of rebirths will be kinder. Perhaps, little by little, over the eons the poor will find a way to atone for their many sins and so earn release from their suffering. Perhaps.

We arrived in Kolkata in 2001. From our beautiful homeland of mountains and lakes, we moved to the edge of a slum, where 30,000 people crowded onto a strip of land 5 km long and 15 meters wide, bordering an inner city railway line. Row after row of tiny brick huts crammed with five or seven or more family members. Few had the space or savings for luxuries like a toilet. The railway track itself sufficed as the place to deposit bodily wastes. Electricity was stolen from the Government by enterprising young men splicing wires into the city lines running nearby. Every 100 meters or so, some entrepreneur had sunk a bore-hole, and so for a few rupees, water from a single hand-pumped well met the needs of hundreds for thirst, for cooking, for washing. In the searing summer, the queues to bathe at these outdoor 'bathroom taps' were long and exhausting. Gambling, alcoholism and violence seemed endemic among the local men. As for most of the women, their low status and limited freedoms kept them from leaving their one-room homes without permission. They were not allowed any financial control independent of their husbands, nor were they to complain when struck for any real or imagined failure in performing their domestic duties.

We spent our first year building relationships and trying to understand the culture of this community, opening our hearts and home to our neighbors. Over time our friendships grew deep roots. As we observed the lives of our friends, we were staggered by the weight the women of this slum had to carry on their shoulders.

While their husbands often drank and gambled, the women worked their fingers to the bone, trying to earn enough income to feed, clothe and educate their children, yet still so many were viewed as inferior chattel to be used and abused at will.

Over these first few months, a burden grew in our hearts to help these women earn a fair income, and with it some respect and autonomy. As we looked around at projects initiated by development organizations and missions, we saw many producing creative craft products, but they still struggled to turn a profit. From this dilemma, we were inspired to open a fair trade outlet in our home country to sell the crafts from various projects and return a decent wage to the women producers.

In 2002, with six women friends from the railway slum, we saw the opening of the Vocational Training Center for the teaching of sewing and papercraft skills (cards, gift bags etc.). Our hope was that this would be a place of healing, wholeness and discipleship, a community of shared lives where women would be empowered to become servant-leaders and where local Indian leaders would emerge and take over the business. In 2003, the Training Center joined with a vibrant local church, and quickly began to expand. Later that year, the ministry linked up with Kolkata University, who now helps tutor and certificate the tailoring course, simultaneously raising its professional standards and offering a much sought after qualification.

Then, in 2005, the local Government demolished the railway slum, something they had been threatening to do for ten long years, but had been kept at bay due to the intense opposition - and at times violence - from the slum dwellers. Facing injury and possible death from the 2,000 police who had been sent to demolish the slum, and tired from a decade of confrontations, the community finally accepted the Government's offer of land on an alternative site for all who owned titles in the slum.

This, of course, left all the families who rented totally destitute. Tears streamed down the faces of those watching as the community of 30,000 was demolished in hours.

Many of the young women working with us had to find

alternative accommodation. Some managed to find a small piece of floor space in the neighboring slum, while others were forced to relocate hours away from places of work and school, and their networks of friends and neighbors.

By 2006, nearly fifty young women were involved in the project and a joyful community had developed. Along with these young women and the local church, we were opening our lives and homes to one another, sharing our needs and food with one another, crying, praying and celebrating with one another, reading Scriptures and worshipping with one another. Acts 2:42-47 had become our model.

Step by step, with no pressure placed on anyone to become a Christian or convert them away from their existing religion or culture, the young women involved were coming to know Jesus. One of the pastors we knew had now begun a small church on the edge of the slum, and regularly visited the girls. Each week, just as the girls were finishing work, these pastors would come and offer to pray for them. Soon, to their amazement, the girls discovered that the pastor's wife had a gift of healing, and they began to experience miraculous recoveries following these prayer times.

Excited by what they were learning and experiencing, the girls began to invite members of their families to receive prayer, study the Scripture, and participate in worship through traditional Indian dance. Slowly the little church planted in the slum has grown and many from this community are preparing themselves to be baptized.

As these women have grown in their thirst to understand Jesus' way, increasing time has been given over to Scripture study, and they wrestle with what it means to apply Kingdom of God principles to every area of life, both their work place and their home life. The level of self-respect that these young women now possess is clearly evident, as is the pride they take in their work. Six women produce 24,000 beautifully hand crafted cards and paper products each year. The larger tailoring wing produce over a thousand sari blankets a year that are sold in fancy boutiques in Europe and Britain.[15] Some of these blankets even made it onto the set of the recent film *Pirates of the Caribbean*, where it was decided they made the ideal cloth from which pirate clothes could be cut!

There are many Kolkatas. There is a living Kolkata and a dying Kolkata. The young women and men in this community, and in the church that has been planted alongside them, are finding life. In a place of despair, in 'the city of joy', a community of joy is emerging.

Love, Violence And Passivity

Dave Andrews

(Delhi, India)

Dave Andrews (one of the Servant's Elders), his wife, Ange, and their family have spent more than thirty years living in intentional communities with marginalized people in Afghanistan, Pakistan, India, Nepal and Australia. His family now lives in Brisbane, Australia, where they established the Waiters Union, a ministry that seeks to build community with marginalized and vulnerable people. Dave is the author of numerous books, including Christi-Anarchy, Not Religion but Love, Building a Better World, *and* Compassionate Community Work.

For more than ten years, Ange and I, along with our two children, lived in the cosmopolitan city of Delhi. The imperial splendour of Rajpath is superb. The quiet beauty of Lodhi Gardens is enchanting. The hustle and bustle on Chandni Chowk is exciting. But it is the people, the millions of people who crowd into the city from all over India, that make Delhi such a dynamic place to live. It is the convergence of Kashmiris, Punjabis, and Rajasthanis, the Nagas, Mizos and Manipuris, the Biharis, Bengalis, and Oriya; the

Telegus, Tamils and Mal-ayalis—vibrant streams forming a great river—that persuaded the classical poet Ghalib to describe Delhi as "the soul in the body of the world."

While we were there, we lived in an intentional multi-ethnic community called Aashiana, which included twenty-one non-Indians and thirty-two Indians. Of the non-Indians, thirteen of us were from Australia, four from England, three from Canada, and one from Germany. Of the Indians, sixteen were from Delhi itself, six from Punjab, five from Goa, three from Maharashtra, two from Tamil Nadu, and one from Andhra Pradesh. Almost half of the marriages were international, and almost all of the marriages (including our own) were cross-cultural. The complexity was further compounded by the fact that we were not only international and crosscultural, but also multi-faith. Twenty-three of us were Christian, five Hindu, two Humanist, one Muslim, one Buddhist and one Jain! At one stage or other, we all actually lived together in the same six bed-roomed house - and, believe it or not, we all absolutely loved it!

As a community, we were enchanted by a vision of having more of heaven come here on earth. We were intoxicated with a passion for God and moved by a compassion for our neighbors. Jesus' Sermon on the Mount became our manifesto.

We welcomed strangers. We shared meals with guests around our table. We ate joy and sorrow. We drank to redemption. We cared for the sick, the addicted and the abused. We gladly shared our wealth with the poor. As a community we were committed to working for justice with marginalised groups of people around the city of Delhi.

As Christians, Jesus was our role model. We also looked to the example of Gandhi as someone who had taken seriously Jesus' teachings and made them work in the Indian context. (Just as Martin Luther King in the American context, had also combined the teachings of Jesus with the tactics of Gandhi, and so moved mountains.)We were committed to his philosophy of using 'soul force' rather than violence or aggression. We were committed to putting the last first, and doing the most with the least. We turned our home into a rehab community for young people addicted to heroin and other drugs, helping them on the condition that they would help others. It wasn't long before we had a large team of recovering addicts from *Sahara* (which is what we called our rehab work) helping us in *Sharan*[16] (which is what we called our development work), doing voluntary work with the poorest of the poor in the slums around the city of Delhi.

Ange and I now look back on this time as a biblical dream come true. We will never forget it. We *were* tasting heaven. An ancient saying etched on a wall of Lal Quila (Shah Jahan's majestic Red Fort in Delhi) seemed to speak out of the mists of history just for us. It read: 'If on earth there is a place of bliss, it is this, it is this, it is this.'

Then one day, all hell broke loose. The Prime Minister, Indira Gandhi, was assassinated by her Sikh bodyguards. People went crazy. They took to the streets.

Wherever they could find Sikhs, they would grab them by their long, uncut hair, hold them down, pour petrol over them and set them alight. Mobs stopped buses and stormed trains, searching for Sikhs, pulling people off at random, and cutting them to pieces as they struggled to escape their captors. The police were completely unprepared. Where they were prepared they were completely outnumbered. We heard of one police inspector in Vasant Vihar who confronted and faced down a mob single-handedly. However, incidents of such courage were exceptional. The police were unable - or unwilling - to do much at all. The mobs ruled the streets.

Wherever they went, these mobs of weapon-wielding maniacs, driven mad by grief and anger and years of suppressed frustration and disempowerment, looted and burned everything they could lay their hands on. Soon billowing columns of smoke rose from vehicles, petrol stations, department stores, factories and houses all over the city. People clambered onto their roofs to witness the sight of buildings all over the city ablaze like thousands of funeral pyres. Within a period of less than twenty-four hours, more than 3,000 Sikhs, who (until then) had been living peacefully with their neighbors for decades, were slaughtered senselessly on the streets of Delhi.

I knew that I could not simply stand by and watch all this horror unfolding around me. I called myself a follower of Jesus, and I had to do *something*. But, *kya kare yaar? What to do?* Up until then we had consciously practiced Gandhi's teaching on *savodaya* (constructive action), but had never had cause to test out his philosophy of satyagraha (non-violent intervention). I felt totally inadequate and terribly afraid. It's one thing to talk about the risks we need to take when we *don't* need to take any; it's another thing to take those risks when we *do* need to take them.

I knew that this was my moment of truth, yet I was so frightened that doing *nothing* seemed infinitely preferable to doing *something* that could plunge me into very real danger. But deeper than the fear, I knew in my spirit that if I didn't stand by my Sikh neighbors it would be a complete contradiction of everything I had ever said about neighbors loving one another and standing by each other in their hour of need. I discussed it with Ange, and we talked it over with our friends in the community.

Yes, we had to do something, and slowly a rough plan began to form in our minds. Luke and Meera Samson decided to stay on in their house in order to support the Sikh families living above and below them in their building. Aashwini, Hoshang and Sundar went to stay with a Hindu neighbor, who had asked for help in protecting two Sikhs staying with him. One of these guys had already been badly beaten, only just escaping from a rampaging mob, and he was trembling with fear.

The rest of us in the Aashiana community decided to make our homes available as sanctuaries for Sikhs seeking refuge. As the word spread, Sikhs fled to us. We closed the windows, drew the curtains, locked the doors, and prayed the mobs would pass us by. Ange remembered an elderly Sikh builder who was living on a building site across the road from our house and sent me to get him. I crept across the road, snuck him back to our house and secreted him deep inside our bedroom.

This was all *good*, but I knew it wasn't really *enough*. Sikhs were being slain left and right, and there was a desperate need for *active*, rather than passive, *non-violent intervention.* But what was *I* to do? I talked it over once more with Ange. Knowing me too well, she said that whatever I decided to do must be guided by God's Spirit and not driven by some deep-seated messianic complex! However, she added that if it was her father, brother or son being killed, she would want someone like me to try and intervene. She gave me her blessing to go.

So I hopped on my motorbike with my friend Tony, and we went in search of Sikhs under siege. I think I had this brilliant idea that we'd race into some mob chasing a Sikh, get ahead of them, pull the victim onto the back of the bike, then accelerate off into the sunset.

But not surprisingly, it didn't actually work out like that. We had just set off on our mission when we rode around a corner and ran straight into a mob of over a hundred people wielding knives and swords, and an assortment of wooden clubs and iron bars. We stopped, took a deep breath to calm our nerves, and walked over to talk to the mob.

'*Namaste. Kya hal hai?*' What are *you* guys doing here? I asked.

'We're here to kill some Sikhs!' they shot back. Then asked, 'What are *you* doing here?'

'I'd rather not say.' I replied.

'Tell us' they insisted.

'You wouldn't believe it even if I told you,' I said.

'Try us,' they pressed.

'Well, believe it or not,' I said, 'we're here to stop you from killing anybody.'

They laughed. I laughed too. It *was* ridiculous to think that there was anything a couple of unarmed men could do to prevent an armed mob going on a rampage.

'Let's see what happens,' they said. 'We are going to wait here for a bus. Check out the passengers and if we get our hands on one of those bastards, we're going to cut him to pieces. It'll be fun to see what you're going to do about that!'

While they waited for a bus, we waited with them. I used the time to chat with them about their families and talk to them about my own wife and children. I hoped that when the moment of confrontation came they would relate to me as a nice man with a wife and two children, rather than as a disposable stranger.

When a bus came along, they jumped aboard and searched high and low—no Sikhs. They got off, disgruntled. Another bus came along, and again they jumped aboard, searched high and low—still no Sikhs. Now, as they got off, their anger turned to rage. They marched to a shopping centre, smashing into the shops and setting them on fire. Then they quickly abandoned the shopping centre and marched up the road towards an estate. It was blood, not loot, they wanted.

We jumped on the motorbike again and raced ahead of the mob to try and organize some neighborhood resistance to the invasion.

'They are going to kill the Sikhs!' I cried.

'Serves them right!' the Hindus replied.

We were wondering what to do next when a cry rang out. The rabble had come across a post box with the name, 'Singh,' printed on it, suggesting Sikhs in residence.

They'd broken into their house, and the family had fled to the patio on the roof, calling for help.

We raced to the spot, pushed our way through the crowd, and took our stand, between the mob and the family, at the bottom of the stairs. We faced the horde with our hands held together in a gesture of peace, pleading, 'Shanti. Shanti.' Peace.

Peace. 'Unko na marna.' Don't hurt them.

The mob broke down the door, busted up the furniture, and threatened to butcher us if we didn't let them through. We were tempted to run, but stood our ground at the bottom of the stairs. They took the petrol cap off our motorbike, threw a match in the petrol tank, set it on fire, and threatened to do the same to us if we didn't let them through. Our hearts were pounding, our palms were sweating and our knees were shaking, but we stayed where we were.

For a moment, our fate hung in the balance. If one of them had hit us, we knew that all of them would have cut us to pieces or set us on fire - like all the other mobs did that day. But they hesitated, and as they hesitated, I could sense the moment of danger building - and then evaporating. They broke ranks, spat curses at us, turned their backs and walked away.

When it was safe, we called out to the family who were still huddled on the roof. They came down the stairs very warily, looking around to make sure the mob had gone. When they saw it was all clear, we hugged one another and then all sat down on the front steps and wept together with relief.

In crises such as these, the Spirit always prompts us to be who, deep-down, we really want to be, and to do what we deeply, truly, madly want to do. If you are like me, you will probably be tempted to think there is nothing you can do. But, in retrospect, I think there is always something we can do if we listen to the still small voice of the Spirit. The little we can do may not make a lot of difference—but then again, it may be the difference between life and death!

Special Section

AFTER THE KHMER ROUGE: FIVE
LIVES OF HOPE AND COURAGE

Kristin Jack

(Phnom Penh, Cambodia)

In this section we have retold (based on interviews) the stories of five TASK[17] staff: how they survived Pol Pot, how they found Jesus, and how they came to work with TASK.

When I think of the most profound, long-run miracles I've seen in Cambodia, I think first of these—and other—Cambodian co-workers, who worked alongside us to establish Servant's health and community development programmes by sacrificially ministering to the poorest and neediest among the slums and squatter settlements of Phnom Penh—those dying of AIDS and TB, the severely malnourished and disabled children, the hundreds of AIDS orphans. These selfless men and women helped us train a younger generation to carry on this work by recruiting and empowering nearly two hundred community workers in poor neighborhoods to take the ministries even closer to the poorest and most desperate.

Then, after ten long years, these men and women took full responsibility for leading and managing the health and development initiatives they'd begun with Servants, birthing TASK, a Government recognized, local Christian NGO.

Every time I watch one of the men or women in TASK ministering love and healing to their own community, to their poorest brothers and sisters, I'm watching something supernatural. Every time I see a sick child cradled in someone's compassionate arms and brought back from the brink of starvation, I know I am witnessing a miracle.

We continually remember before our God and Father your work produced by faith, your labor prompted by love, and your endurance inspired by hope in our Lord Jesus Christ...Our gospel came to you not simply with words, but with power, and with the Holy Spirit and deep conviction. You know how we lived among you for your sake. You became imitators of us and of the Lord despite severe suffering, and you welcomed the message with the joy given by the Holy Spirit. And so you became a model to all the believers in the region."

(1 Thessalonians 1:2-7)

A Family Torn Apart, A Life Restored

Sina Suos

Sina Suos is a soft spoken man with large, almond-brown eyes that sparkle when he laughs, but fill with profound sadness in unguarded moments. His gentle, servant heart—once so broken—has been moved by the needs of his people, and he is responding with practical, healing compassion.

When the Khmer Rouge regime took over Cambodia, Sina Suos

was twenty-five years old, married, with three daughters. Like so
many others, he was put to work toiling from early morning till late
at night in Pol Pot's rice fields. After work, he was required to sit
through an hour of Khmer Rouge propaganda. His wife endured
the same routine, and his children were watched by elderly "child
supervisors." Sina says, "At the time, I thought I would die soon,
because they never provided us with enough food. And I began to
plan to run away."

In 1979, the Khmer Rouge moved Sina and his wife and
daughters into separate work camps. Knowing that he had nothing
else to lose, he fled for Thailand. "I didn't know where to go, what
path to take," Sina remembers. "I just ran." On his journey, Sina
joined up with others who were trying to reach the border, and
they were able to help one another. Tragically, before reaching the
border safely, they all found themselves trapped in an unmarked
minefield. Sina watched helplessly as his friends tripped mines and
died in agony. Somehow, he stumbled on and made it to safety in
neighboring Thailand.

Upon reaching Nong Chan, Thailand, Sina found work for fifty
cents a day, portering food and goods back and forth across the Thai
border, where he met some old friends, who generously supplied
him with money and food. After some time, UN workers arrived
with relief supplies, providing people with fifteen kilograms of rice
and three cans of fish per week.

During this time, Sina regularly wrote letters to his wife, hoping
to be reunited if the regime ever came to an end. But years later,
Sina discovered that his wife had been told that he was dead, and
in a desperate situation, she had remarried another man, thus
permanently wrenching apart their family.

In 1979, after someone in the refugee camp shared the gospel
with Sina and gave him a copy of the New Testament, he decided
to follow Christ and began to live with a new zeal and passion.

From 1980 to 1993, Sina worked with Christian mission groups
providing practical care in the refugee camp, and it was here he
received training in basic health management. When Glenn and
Siobahn Miles moved to Phnom Penh in 1993 to launch Servants,

Sina joined them, taking on the role of buying medical supplies and then organizing immunization programs amongst the Mein Chey slums, where hundreds of children were in danger of dying or being crippled by preventable diseases. Due to Sina's efforts in walking the dusty alleys to visit families in their shacks, and his determination to cajole Government staff to reach out to these families, immunization rates in the Mein Chey slums climbed from 20 percent to nearly 90 percent.

More recently Sina has begun an initiative to reach the growing numbers of children and teenagers using street drugs, especially glue and amphetamines, in the Mein Chey area. A market garden has been developed, and life skills and vocational training classes are being taught. Youth workers from local churches help run the programs, including drug prevention education taught to at-risk families and to the wider community.

That's Where They Executed My Husband

Sophat Nourn

(Project Manager, Church and Community Development)

Sophat Nourn is something of a rarity for an older Cambodian: she was born into a Christian home and committed her life to serving Christ as a young teenager in 1962. The vast majority of Christians now in Cambodia have been converted since freedom of religion became possible in 1991. Probably 95 percent of those who were Christians prior to Pol Pot were killed under his murderous regime, which tried to extinguish all traces of religion.

Sophat Nourn was born into a stable and loving family in 1951. After training as a midwife, she married a good Christian man, and together they had three children.

They looked forward to a long and contented life together.

But when Sophat was twenty-five, Pol Pot's fanatical movement took over Cambodia, and the regime separated her from her husband and children.[18] She was permitted to see her three young children once a week, but five months into the regime, her five-year-old girl died of an untreated illness. But she was only allowed to meet with her young husband once a month, up until the time of his execution for some trumped up misdemeanor. Several years later, while we in Servants and TASK were all enjoying a staff picnic just outside Phnom Penh, Sophat sadly pointed across the gentle river where children were now swimming and playing and whispered to us, "Over there on that bank—that's where they executed my husband."

In the intense heat, Sophat worked in the rice fields every day from 5.00am in the morning till 6.00pm at night. After a short break for rice soup and indoctrination, she would be sent back to the fields with the others in her camp until 10.00 pm. About midnight, when she thought her guards were asleep, she would risk her life and slip back out into the fields, gleaning and scavenging for any food she could find to bring back to her two children. It would usually be 1.00 am before she could finally lay down to sleep, allowing her only a few short hours rest before the guards would order everyone back to work at 4.00 or 5.00 am. But Sophat never forgot to pray to God, knowing that it was only his grace that could keep her alive.

On January 7, 1979, Vietnamese forces invaded Cambodia and brought the Khmer Rouge regime to an end. Four days later, weeping tears of joy, Sophat was reunited with her two surviving children. Together, they moved back to Phnom Penh near the area known as Toul Tom Pong.

Soon, Sophat and three friends took over an old, abandoned hospital building, where they provided care for those who had been brutalized and starved by the regime. Eventually the Government provided staff and medical supplies, and the old building became one of the few full-fledged hospitals in the city.

After working at the hospital for four and a half years, Sophat moved to the Thai border, hoping to emigrate to the United States. Soon, she realized that God was really calling her to minister in Cambodia, rather than emigrate, and so she continued to live on at the Thai border camps, working as a nurse and serving as an elder in a church established there. Finally, in 1992, she was repatriated back to Cambodia and worked with the UN to get the national elections underway. Through her pastor, she connected with Servants' disabled children's program (The Little Conquerors or TLC),[19] where she began working as a nurse in 1996 and soon progressed to program coordinator.

In a karma-based culture like Cambodia's, disability is often viewed with shame. When the TLC program started in 1994, these children were often isolated and hidden away from public gaze. As well as providing medicine and physical therapy, TLC provides a venue where families can talk openly about disability to encourage and support each other. With Sophat's guidance, many of these families have since come to know the God who loves them, and so no longer view their disabled children as burdens, but rather as precious gifts. Sophat loves to be a part of the physical and spiritual healing of the children she works with, sharing Christ's love for them as she cares for their bodies and their hearts.

The Long Journey From Buddhist Monk To Rice Farmer, From Captive To Healer

Or Ee

(Community Health Project Manager)

With his neat, silver-grey hair and confident smile, Mr. Or Ee looks like a natural leader. Presently, much of his time as a Medical Assistant is spent counseling and comforting those with HIV/AIDS and organizing their on-going care. But over the course of his life, Or Ee has been many things: Buddhist monk, school teacher, suspect intellectual, porter, quarry worker, carpenter, Khmer Rouge captive, hospital administrator, Red

THE SOUND OF WORLDS COLLIDING

Cross administrator, UN worker—and now, disciple of Christ.

Or Ee was born in the rural province of Takeo in 1950. His parents, like most Cambodians, were rice farmers, who balanced hard labor with rich community and friendship. After an arduous season of planting and harvesting, there was always the off-season, which was filled with ceremonies, celebrations and visits to family and friends.

At twenty, Or Ee left home to study to become a Buddhist monk - a common progression for young Cambodian men in those days. When political and military tension started to build in 1970, he moved to another pagoda near his family's home so he could help his parents on their rice farm.

In 1975, when the Khmer Rouge overran the country, Or Ee quickly left his position as a monk and attempted to live in such a way that his education and Buddhist background would not be discovered.[20] He took a job that required him to transport fifty-kilogram bags of rice on his back for forty meters, a cycle which he repeated fifty times a day. He speaks of this as being "the good life," when he was given plenty of rice to eat and worked for only eight hours a day. After six months, he was sent back to Takeo province with a work gang to help dig a dam and was able to resume helping his parents on their rice farm.

In 1976, his parents moved closer to the Vietnamese border, and Or Ee was sent to the Sihanoukville area to work in a warehouse. A year later, after digging into Or Ee's background and discovering that he had been an educated monk, the Khmer Rouge labeled him 'an intellectual' and accused him and his family of being enemies of the 'people's revolution.' Suspicious of his every move, the regime assigned him to Group 19, one of the harshest work sites in the province. For two long years, he worked eleven hours a day - drilling and breaking up rocks for building projects,[21] planting fruit and vegetables - then attended mandatory Khmer Rouge indoctrination sessions, and then performed guard duty through the night. By working hard, staying silent, and assenting to the Khmer Rouge propaganda, he survived - though just barely, as his meals were limited to a plate of bor-bor (thin rice soup) twice each day.

While the Vietnamese invasion in 1979 liberated Cambodia from the Khmer Rouge, the night sky was continually lit up by exploding artillery shells. Or Ee fled towards Thailand, first buying space on a boat heading towards the border, then trekking on foot through the forest with minimal food supplies. On the month-long journey, he encountered many other Cambodians who had been severely injured by land mines. Everyone shared what little they had to help one another, and at last, he staggered into Site 8, a Khmer Rouge controlled border camp, where UN workers fed him and cared for him. Because he was competent in French and English, owned a medical dictionary and had learned some medical skills in the pagoda[22], he soon became a vital part of the border camp community, working for the International Red Cross from 1981-1993, re-training as Medical Assistant, and eventually serving as hospital administrator.

When the United Nations began repatriating Cambodian refugees from the border camps back into Cambodia in the early 1990s, Or Ee got a job with the United Nations (UNTAC), helping run Cambodia's first democratic elections. In 1994, Or Ee met Glenn Miles, and eventually took on a role for Servants, liaising with the local Government hospital.

Although Or Ee had heard the message of Christ's love in the refugee camp, where Christians were very actively helping the refugee community, he was most deeply impacted by seeing his Servants co-workers' faith being lived out daily in service to the poor and the sick. After about a year with Servants, he committed himself to following Jesus and was baptized in a local river by his friend, Kristin.

In addition to being a senior leader, Or Ee is involved with treating those with TB and AIDS, and in heading up TASK's Community Health response for the very poor.[23] Though he works with some of the most desperate and broken people in his community, he loves this role because it enables him "to help those who suffer, and to help them find hope, just as I have found hope."

From Moto-Taxi Driver To Gifted Leader

Pauv Prom

(TASK Director)

*When you first meet Pauv, the director of TASK, you might wonder
how someone who looks so young gained the wisdom and vision necessary
for such responsibility. And you are right to wonder, for the story of Pauv's
progression into the role has been one of God's grace all the way.*

Pauv was three years old when Pol Pot took control of
Cambodia. His parents were simple rice farmers, and because their
first-born had died in childhood, Pauv took on the responsibilities
of the oldest child in the family.

During the Pol Pot regime, Pauv's family fared better than
many Cambodians, probably because of their simple rural identity.
His father was appointed as the cook for his village[24], and Pauv
often spent time sitting at his father's feet as he cooked meals.
He even had the privilege of tasting chicken meat occasionally,
which was an unheard of luxury for those living under the regime.
Nevertheless, five of Pauv's siblings died of untreated illnesses
during this time.

Pauv was eight when the Khmer Rouge were driven from power.
He began attending school in a 'building' constructed from packed
dirt, which crumbled away with each rainfall, and continually
reeked of dampness and mildew. Without furniture or supplies, the
students sat on the ground, using palm leaves for chairs and their
knees as desks.

After completing high school in 1992, Pauv moved to Phnom
Penh, where he found work as a moto-taxi driver.[25] Having picked
up some English, Pauv began to specialize in ferrying foreigners,
often waiting on Sundays outside the International Church,
since there were always plenty of customers. Soon, he met Jenny
Searles, an Australian woman who was the administrator of
Servants in Cambodia at that time. Impressed with his sharp,

honest personality, she took him on as her personal moto-taxi driver. As Pauv continued to prove himself, Jenny began to teach him the basics of her administrative work. In 1994, he moved from personal moto-driver to full-time Servants Co-Administrator[26], where he mastered an array of computer and bookkeeping skills, and showed real flair in the way he related to other staff.

As Jenny worked with Pauv or traveled on the back of his moto, she shared the gospel with him. Having observed that there were many people who called themselves Christians, but who did not appear to live out the words of Jesus, he had many doubts and questions. But he began to read the Bible, and he came to recognize - and believe in - Jesus as the source of hope and justice.

Only a few years ago, Pauv was a poor country boy possessing little more than a big smile, running a motor-scooter and ferrying foreigners to and from their strange religious services. Now, drawn by his love for the poor and suffering, Pauv has helped construct wells for the poor communities in his home province, and he took great joy in helping to rebuild the school he attended as a child. These days, with thirty-five Khmer staff under his direction at TASK, he continues to demonstrate an outstanding ability to 'lead through serving' - a trait that for too long has been tragically absent in Cambodia. By providing a role model of humble, compassionate and determined leadership, Pauv is leading the vanguard of young Khmer leaders emerging to help rebuild their nation.

Pain Turned To Love

Kimchhoeun Chhim

(Children's Worker and Counselor)

Kimchhoeun works with HALO, TASK's program for children who have been orphaned by AIDS. By placing these children in homes with their extended families, they are kept out of orphanages and off the streets. Kimchhoeun is a gifted youth counselor, and leads a team of older teenagers from HALO in an income generating craft venture known as 'Slumlight.'[27]

Born in 1979, Kimchhoeun Chmim was the oldest of six children. At the time of her birth, her mother was a housewife, and her father was a policeman who later branched out into a private business.

Kimchhoeun's education progressed smoothly from grades 1-8 because her family's earnings were stable enough to support her schooling. But the failure of her father's business when she was in grade 9 cut her high school education short. Her father had been a transporter of clothing from Cambodia to Vietnam, but one wet season the fabric was ruined when one of the trucks slid off the road into a muddy river.

Her father sold their trucks and some of the family jewellery in an attempt to pay back loans, but the family had plummeted too deeply into poverty by this time.

So both Kimchhoeun's parents left home in an attempt to dig for precious stones in the North West of the country, leaving Kimchhoeun and her siblings to fend for themselves. As a fifteen-year-old, Kimchhoeun found herself in charge of the family.

Unfortunately, this business venture also failed, with her parents robbed several times while prospecting, and so they soon returned home, poorer than ever.

Back home, her father fell into a deep sense of shame over the poverty he and the family had fallen into. He began to avoid his family and his community as much as possible. Now he rarely came to the house, and became an absent father to his children. In the meantime, her mother scraped money together by making and selling rice meals. But this earned very little, leaving Kimchhoeun and her siblings constantly short of the money they needed for food and education.

But Kimchhoeun persevered in her studies, as she was determined to finish college and then pursue her dream of going to medical school. She woke up at three o'clock in the morning to help her mother sell, then studied for the rest of the day.

Life was hard, a constant struggle with never enough time or money. Then, in the middle of grade 11, Kimchhoeun discovered that her father had taken on a second wife. Pain and a sense of betrayal overwhelmed her. Too despairing to think about her own future anymore, she quit her studies and dropped out of high school, now convinced that her younger brothers and sisters would have no education unless she found a job and saved money for them.

Kimchhoeun, now eighteen, found a job at a Korean-owned burger place. Her boss at the restaurant was a Christian, as was one of her neighbors. Both of them discussed their faith openly. Because Kimchhoeun had heard that Christians stood against Buddhism and ridiculed Buddha as an "idol," she hated Christians and would not allow the name of Jesus to be spoken in her presence.

Her father then began visiting the house again because he was having problems with his second wife. Angry at the way her and her siblings had been treated, Kimchhoeun felt herself burning with hatred toward her parents, especially her father; the affection and devotion of her childhood was gone. She could not stand being in the presence of her father; the very sight of him repulsed her. He often came home to visit on Sundays, and she was so desperate to get away from him that she agreed to go to church with her aunt one Sunday.

The sermon that day was about the fruit of the Spirit—about joy, love and forgiveness — and it was like a mirror being held up, enabling Kimchhoeun to see how much hate was within her.

Thirsting for more, and feeling drawn to the friendliness and love of the church congregation, she decided to come back the next Sunday.

Kimchhoeun's heart began to be softened and transformed as she reached out for this Jesus. Even though no one had taught her or shown her how, she began to pray, crying out with all her heart. Her father soon found out about her new faith. He was furious and confronted her, saying that she must "choose between her father and this Jesus." He commanded her to stop attending church. Her heart had been changed, and Kimchhoeun no longer felt her previous hatred towards her father, but nor could she deny Christ. She continued going to church. Her pastor, meanwhile, had sold her a new Bible for $1 (its original price being $5). She put this Bible, along with some Christian booklets she owned, on her bedside table. One day, her father stormed into her room and demanded an answer to his question, "your father or Jesus?" Still unwilling to renounce her Savior, Kimchhoeun responded, "Yes you are my father, but Jesus is Christ!" Enraged, her father hurled her Bible and booklets across the room, struck her, and forced her out of the house screaming at her that she was no longer his daughter.

Kimchhoeun gathered her belongings and took a moto-taxi to her church, the only place she could think to go for food or shelter. At the church, though, the members insisted that she should go back home and try and repair the relationship with her father in spite of his intense anger.

So Kimchhoeun returned home and begged her father to take her back in. He did allow her shelter, and for the months that followed she doused him with as much daughterly care, attention and love as was possible for her. She carried his briefcase for him when he came home; she offered him water; she massaged him when he was fatigued.

She prayed and prayed — along with her church — that he would accept her faith. And finally, after a few months, her father gave her his official permission to attend church. She and the church rejoiced at the way God had granted her request.

Soon, her pastor noticed that she had a talent for studying and understanding the Bible, and encouraged her to go to Bible school. She took the required examinations and got very high marks, but the school would not allow her to enrol until she received the consent of her parents.

Her father refused to let her study there. Once again there was the process of fervent praying. This lasted for two weeks, until finally her father hand wrote an agreement that he would give her his support. Once more God had dramatically turned his heart around.

From the years 2000-2003, Kimchhoeun attended Phnom Penh Bible School and gained a diploma in Christian ministries and in Christian education.

Shortly after graduation, a friend showed her a job announcement for a young Christian woman to work with TASK in its HALO project for AIDS orphans, and urged her to apply. The opportunity seemed perfect, as she had long had a passion to work with young people like this. Kimchhoeun soon began work with HALO, and loves the way it enables her to get so close to the children and understand what they are going through. Having experienced pain and trauma in her own life, she knows she has something to offer them.

Several years later, when Kimchhoeun fell in love with Kimsrun, who was also a Christian, they asked their parent's permission to wed. Even though the parents hadn't arranged this match (as is the norm in Cambodia), they were happy to let the marriage go ahead, so long as it was celebrated with a traditional Buddhist ceremony. But Kimchhoeun and Kimsrun were determined to have a Christian ceremony. Both sets of parents refused. Kimchhoeun and Kimsrun said, "Then we will wait, because we don't want to get married until we can have a ceremony that really honors Jesus."

As the months stretched out longer and longer, and it became clear that this stalemate could go on forever, both sets of parents relented, and allowed Kimchhoeun and Kimsrun to arrange their own ceremony.

After the vows, both Kimchhoeun and Kimsrun knelt down and washed their parent's feet, a traditional Khmer wedding ritual that demonstrates the children's deep respect for their parents.

As Kimchhoeun gently stroked the lotus-strewn water across her father's feet, his face crumpled, and he asked for the M.C's microphone.

Struggling to get his words out through his tears, he told the congregation how proud he was of his daughter and the person she had become, and he thanked those present for the way they had supported her and helped shape her life. Kimchhoeun, listening at his feet, had to keep wiping away her own tears, as did every other guest present that day.

Gifts From The Slum

Sarah Aulie

(Phnom Penh, Cambodia)

Sarah Aulie, a young photographer from Wheaton College, visited Servants in Cambodia for one life-changing month at the end of 2003. Here she sketches a picture of the hope she discovered in the most unexpected place—the faces of people dying of AIDS.

I.

Sarim, a Cambodian nurse around my age who works for Servants visiting AIDS patients in their homes, arrives with a suitcase full of medicine. Another Khmer woman arrives with her Bible.

The patient cannot breathe and I am sure she is going to die.

Sarim gives her a medication that helps her lungs expand, and her breathing becomes less labored, more natural. The Khmer woman opens her Bible and begins reading. The three of us lay hands on the dying woman and pray for her. I see Jesus erase the fear from the woman's face and soften the lines around her mouth.

II.

The room waits for her to die. The floor is swept. Flowers stand in the corner, heads bent. Three women sit with their back against the wall. A framed picture of the dying woman when she still had flesh on her face hangs above us.

A monk wrapped in orange robes, brilliant against dark skin, waits outside the door to prepare the last ceremony over the body.

I crouch low and touch the bone of the dying woman's arm. She stares in my direction, this corpse, but she is blind. She lost her eyesight just a few days ago, Sarim tells me. She speaks to the woman-skeleton in Khmer, explaining who is touching her arm.

The woman's fingers struggle to find the edge of the blanket and push it back. Then, summoning all her strength, she presses her hands together in the Khmer formal greeting, a silent expression written into Cambodian culture of humbling yourself before another person. This gesture of humanity turns the skeleton into a woman.

"Akoon," I cry out. "Thank you." With all the dignity she could muster, this dying woman has humbled herself before us and, with close-pressed hands, given us her last gift.

III.

Sok, an AIDS home care nurse for Servants, winds her way past brothels, down narrow garbage strewn lanes to Mi Sa's house.

The room is lit by fractured rays of light coming in through the floorboards. Mi Sa, a ten-year-old boy, crouches over a camping stove. The growing batch of rice in his pot begins to push its way up from under the lid and the room is filled with the scent of cooked rice. In the corner, on a wood bed, lies his father, a heap of bones draped in skin. The father groans and pulls himself to his side, revealing a red sore that spreads down his back.

Sok slips off her shoes and climbs onto the wooden bed. She touches the man's face and skull, dips a cloth into cold water and begins to bathe him, washing his sore.

I hang back in the shadows, afraid of his bones, afraid of his sore, watching Mi Sa.

When the rice is finished, he pokes at the pregnant pot and eats at the white fringe that sticks to his spoon. His sister starts to cry. He balances her on his hip and brings her into the front room. There, by the light from the doorway, he rocks his baby sister, feeding her white formula from a bottle.

Another man with Servants opens his Khmer Bible and begins to read in a gentle voice. The man's face, riddled with lines, seemed to soften.

My attention is still absorbed by Mi Sa, whose mother has left to find work in a factory. He is so good with his little sister. So responsible. Is it strange for him to see his father reduced to something so ugly? I wonder, or is it just as much a part of his life as cooking rice on the camping stove?

"Sok, what will happen to Mi Sa?" I ask as we leave.

They have not been forgotten.

"All of the orphans from the AIDS home care patients are the children of Project HALO."[28]

IV.

The past week I've been feeling uncommonly exhausted, maybe because of the heat.

I thought I would hate visiting AIDS patients. I mean, really, how depressing is it to visit people who are going to die and you can do nothing about it? I have no medical training. I'm clueless about Khmer culture. I'm just one silly girl who thought she'd pop over to Cambodia for a good ol' "cultural experience" (good grief!). All the doctors and nurses and relief workers here are working against time. I watch them hand out packets of medicine or bowls of soup, but all of that is just tiding them over, buying more time. The foreign aid pouring into this country will eventually be exhausted; the missionary doctors will go back home. Then what?

That's the way I've been thinking the past few days: "What's the point? They're going to die anyways." Every single patient we visited this morning and every patient we will visit this afternoon is going to die[29].

But this morning, as I watched the fear vanish from that dying woman's face and Mi Sa's father's face soften after prayer, hope was restored. I had been feeling like God was far away, that he might have forgotten all about this place. But this morning I realized that he's been here all along.

Escaping The Brothel

Rita Schreier-Reist[30]

(Phnom Penh)

Rita Schreier-Riest began working with Servants in Phnom Penh in 1994, using her nursing skills to run a brothel clinic that Servants had been asked to start by local hospital staff.[31] After several years of ministry, she returned to Switzerland, where she is involved with the Servants team in Switzerland with her husband, Marcus. They will be returning to Asia in the near future to resume ministry amongst the poor.

Srey Neang[32]

Working in the brothel clinic[33] each week, I met many young women, but Srey Neang was very beautiful and unusually determined. Within a few weeks of working in these brothels, life disappeared from the eyes of most girls, and an air of heavy defeat hung over them. But Srey Neang was different.

When I first met her, she had only been in the brothel three or four weeks, and she had been forced there against her will. Many girls were lured from their rural homes by middle-men or women - often their own relatives - with promises of a high paying job in a restaurant or some other branch of the hospitality industry.

Once away from friends and neighbors and brought into the
city, where they knew no one, the girls would be sold into a brothel,
where they were often told that they had been 'bought' by the
brothel owner for a large sum of money, and that they could not
leave until the debt was worked off by servicing customers. The
girls would be locked up, and if they refused to comply, they would
be starved, beaten or drugged.

"I want to get out," she whispered to me during our weekly
clinic. "Can you help me get out?" Often we talked with girls
about escaping, but the threat of punishment and their own sense
of inertia meant few were willing to risk it. But although she was
only seventeen, there was a steely determination in Srey Neang's
eyes and voice. I rapidly tried to weigh up the risks. If she was
caught trying to escape, she would be punished and perhaps moved
to another brothel. But if she stayed, she faced the slow death of
her spirit, her heart, and finally her body. If I was caught helping
her, the brothel owners might force our clinic to close, though this
was unlikely since we had been given grudging permission from
local Government officials [34]. But if I didn't help her, I would have
to live with the knowledge that I had refused her plea for help.
So I quickly tried to think of a plan that would enable me to get
her outside the brothel without arousing suspicion. "I will ask for
you to come to our Women's Health Clinic in Deum Sleng village
at lunch today, and from there I can get you to a safe house," I
whispered back.

I approached the brothel owner with our story, trying to sound
as casual and routine as I could. "I need to take Srey Neang to
our village clinic for some more treatment. She has some serious
'women's health problems,'[35] and I don't have the right medicines
with me. If she meets me there, I will have the right medicines and
can treat her properly." The brothel owner was relatively young,
but the ravages of pain and hardness were eating away at what
once had been features of deep beauty.

As a sex worker herself, she knew all the tricks, all the angles, and
a look of deep cynicism filled her narrowing eyes. She explained to

me how much she'd paid for Srey Neang, reminding me what a valuable asset she was. "All the more reason you should look after her health," I reminded her.

As soon as the clinic in the brothel was over, I made my way to our Women's Health Clinic, which was based in decaying rooms we borrowed from the local authorities. In reality, it was an empty room, and the only medicines were those I carried with me in my bag or went and bought from nearby pharmacies. As I bumped along the pot-holed streets of Phnom Penh on the back of a moto-dup (motor scooter taxi), something felt strange. Anxiously, I craned my neck to scan the road behind me. My heart lifted as I made out the figure of Srey Neang on the back of a motor-dup maybe 20 meters behind me. She had made it out of the brothel! But my euphoria turned to horror as further back I could see the brothel owner, trailing Srey Neang.

Over the next thirty minutes a bizarre chase unfolded as I directed my moto down alleys and through backstreets, trying to keep Neang in tow but shake off the brothel owner and her driver. Around and around the southern part of Phnom Penh we wound, turning sharply, slowing then suddenly accelerating, but to no avail.

Every time I thought we'd shaken her off, she would reappear again, locked onto our tail. Anger and frustration boiled inside me. Had one of the other girls heard our whispered conversation? Had our story been so obvious? Running out of ideas and time, we finally pulled up at the clinic in Deum Sleng. As I climbed off my moto, Neang's bike appeared. Then, a few seconds later, the motor bike with the brothel owner appeared behind her.

I had planned to quickly whisk Srey Neang from here to a safe house run by another Christian organization in the city. Naively, I had thought once I had her physically outside the brothel, the rest would be straight forward. But now, I had to come up with another plan. I started talking to Neang about her 'women's health problem', handing her some medications and trying to bluff my way through. I said I had decided it was even more serious than I had first thought. "We need to make another appointment, and this time at the local hospital, where I can get you more serious treatment. Please come there." We set up a new appointment time. Fear and confusion filled Neang's eyes. The brothel owner's eyes narrowed with suspicion.

My own mind was whirling—planning, praying, hoping.

When the time of the appointment at the hospital came, Srey Neang never arrived. When I returned to the brothel clinic the next day, there was no sign of her.

None of the other girls knew where she was, nor was the brothel owner there to question. I prayed that Neang had run away and escaped all by herself, but was haunted by the horrible alternative: that she'd been sold to another brothel in a more secure location. What could I have done differently I wondered? Should I have offered to buy Neang off the owner when she told me the price, even though I knew that handing money to a brothel owner was a poor strategy since it reinforced, rather than undermined, the whole sex industry economy? But I felt profoundly sad and powerless. What had become of Srey Neang? What would become of all the Srey Neang's I saw each week?

Srey Kim Eng

I was shocked when I met Kim, who was extraordinarily beautiful and young—only fourteen[36]. When I first saw her she had only just arrived in the brothel, and they did their best to keep her hidden from me. This was the usual procedure, keeping new girls locked up until their bodies and souls were so broken they wouldn't even want to escape. Each time the brothel owner saw me coming, Kim would be hustled inside and hidden away.

But during one of my clinics, Kim managed to slip alongside me and initiate a conversation. "Big sister, I believe in Jesus too," she whispered. "Please pray for me, so that I can get out of here. I have to run away." My stomach knotted and my eyes misted over, I found it hard to concentrate through the rest of that clinic. "Oh God," I cried silently, "how can I get her out?"

"Be careful, Kim. They are watching you and they are watching me. But I will come back for you. I will think of something," I told her.

WHOLISM

That afternoon I caught a moto straight to the ECPAT (End Child Prostitution in Asian Tourism[37]) office and pleaded for their help. The next day, one of their trusted staff entered the brothel, posing as a typical Cambodian male customer. He told them he wanted their youngest girl and was lead to Kim's room, a box-like cubicle made from plywood. In hushed, urgent whispers, they arranged a place to meet that afternoon and how she could get there without being caught.

When Kim never arrived, the rescuer from ECPAT became frantic in his efforts to find her. He returned to the brothel and asked to see Kim again, but she had been transferred to a more secure place, and nobody would tell him where.

The news of the failed rescue and Kim's disappearance overwhelmed me with grief and despair. ECPAT sent more undercover workers into the brothel to try and glean information; they widened their investigation and talked to everyone they knew about this particular brothel. But after two weeks of searching, they hit a stone wall. "This network of brothels is like an extended prison. There is no way for us to get to the inside of it—and no way for those inside to get out. And Rita, you need to be careful. There are important people profiting from this—people who are prepared to be ruthless in protecting their interests." Until that moment I had believed that this brothel was nothing but a spare change earner for the local police.

In spite of this - and so many other truly hopeless circumstances, I knew that God wanted me to keep hope alive for Srey Neang, Srey Kim and all the other girls who came to the clinic. Even when I despaired for these girls I had come to love and care about, I knew that I had to hold on to my hope of who God is, that He sees these girls, that He hears their cries (and mine), that He grieves for their suffering, and that He loves them and longs to transform their shame into joy.

Srey Song Kim

I met Srey Song on the road leading into the brothel alley, where she was waiting to speak with me. She was nearly twenty, a little older than the other girls, and the fact that she was allowed to

119

stand there, unescorted, made me realize that she had won herself some freedom. I glanced at her obviously pregnant belly and understood that she was a less valuable asset to her 'owners' now. Her obvious pregnancy would deter customers. It was a miracle she hadn't been forced to abort the child, the most common way of resolving this 'problem' and getting girls back to work.

Song was a country girl, from the rural province of Prey Veng, a rice growing area maybe 150 kilometers from the city, and her simple dress and simple speech made that obvious. She'd been tricked into leaving home with the promise of 'good work' and had been forced into a brothel in the main township of Prey Veng province, where she'd been raped and become pregnant. Later, she'd been sold into this brothel in Phnom Penh, where the cycle of abuse began all over again. She was desperate to get out, but didn't know how or where she'd go. She owned absolutely nothing, and was completely penniless. This was her second brothel.

I contacted some friends of mine from another Christian rehabilitation shelter for sex workers and arranged a meeting for Song with one of their social workers.

After all the failures and heartbreaks I'd been through, I was amazed that she was allowed to walk out of the brothel to this appointment, where the social worker transported her to the Rehabilitation Center/safe house.

During Song's time at the Centre, she safely delivered a beautiful, healthy girl. Miraculously, blood tests revealed that neither Song nor her baby had been infected with HIV/AIDS. In the shelter, Song grew physically and emotionally stronger and healthier. And as she heard the stories of Jesus - he who had welcomed sex workers - she decided to trust him for the rehabilitation of her whole life. This broken, bewildered girl began to glow with hope as she realized that neither her identity nor her fate were predestined for her.

After a few months in the shelter, Song decided that it was time to try and go home. With the shelter's help, she contacted her parents, telling them that she wanted to return. Very often, families refuse to have their unmarried daughters with children back, since they are seen as a source of shame and embarrassment.[38] But Song's parents seemed overjoyed to hear from her again, and welcomed her back with open arms - another miracle. Rather than returning to her village in shame, Song returned with joy, knowing she had experienced miracles. With every neighbor and relative, every friend that would listen, she shared the story of Jesus, who had given her new life, new hope, a second chance.

When I was with the girls at the clinic, God often reminded me of the hope I had felt in the midst of my own darkness and despair, during my own difficult times as a child and then as a young woman. I felt that God had allowed me to experience those past feelings of powerlessness and shame so that I could now lift these young girls up to Christ with a hope that reached beyond this present pain.[39]

Impersonating The American Ambassador:
Concluding Reflections On Wholism

Kristin Jack

So they called them and commanded them not to speak at all nor teach in the name of Jesus. But Peter and John answered and said to them, "Whether it is right in the sight of God to listen to you more than to God, you judge. For we cannot but speak of the things which we have seen and heard."

(Acts 4:18-20)

We'd been asleep for a couple of hours when the ringing of our phone jerked us awake. As I fumbled around on the chair beside our bed for the phone, I could hear the excited voices of people running along the road outside and the noise of vehicles bumping over its many potholes. By my watch I could see it was half past midnight.

"Are you guys okay?" the caller asked. Fleur was a friend of ours who lived about four kilometres west of our riverside slum, *Chbaa Ampou.*

"Yeah, what's wrong?" I replied.

"We can see a huge fire burning on your side of the river. I think you had better check it out!"

I peered through the thin bars that covered the windows of our house and was stunned to see the sky glowing orange and red. A huge swathe of Chbaa Ampou was up in flames. We could hear horns beeping, people yelling and motor scooters buzzing back and forth. We soon discovered that our neighborhood was not in immediate danger. The blaze was confined to a thick band of the poorest and most densely packed houses in the slum, which ran the length of the river bank.

As I walked among the sea of ashes and twisted sheets of iron the next morning, I learned that over 900 homes had been destroyed, and almost 6,000 people were homeless. Miraculously, only one resident had been killed as the fire quickly leapt between the closely packed thatch and timber houses. Many had escaped the flames by leaping into the nearby Bassac river.

Dazed and uncertain, people were using their bare hands to dig through the black ash and smouldering debris, trying to salvage cutlery, a pot, or a plate or two. Throughout the day, they remained camped on their little burnt-out plots, protecting whatever possessions they had been able to salvage.

Anger and fear swirled in the air as the story circulated that the fire had been started deliberately by Government agents. A group of young men claimed they had seen a flare fired into the slum from a boat on the river. We all knew how keen the Government was to clear this slum away as part of their 'city beautification program', and we had heard rumours that this part of *Chbaa Ampou* was earmarked to become a riverside promenade so that the middle-classes would have something more beautiful to look at when they drove past.

Twenty-four hours later, a second fire broke out in *Phum Tonle Bassac*, another slum on the opposite bank of the river, forcing out an equally large number of residents.

The day following that fire, trucks promptly arrived to ship the newly homeless to a Government relocation site: an empty block of abandoned rice paddies 25 kilometres from the city, where they were dumped with no shelter, no infrastructure, and no amenities.

Because we lived nearby and had been working in Chbaa Ampou for many years, Servants had a strong network of relationships in the fire area, and so we took the lead in coordinating the emergency response, pulling together resources from larger NGO's already in Cambodia and from overseas. With our Khmer co-workers, we surveyed the fire area, talking with families and community representatives, estimating needs and numbers, and trying to work out how to respond. For many people, the situation was absolutely desperate: they had lost every single thing they owned - assets, savings, and even their meagre food stores had been turned to ash.

In coordination with several other NGO's in Phnom Penh, and with churches based in the burnt-out area, we began to assemble emergency food and household goods that would keep people going till they could get back to work, since the neighborhood economy had been destroyed, too.

We were amazed by how quickly the emergency aid came together, providing enough to meet all the victim's immediate needs. But as we were liaising with local officials, the Government issued an edict: *There was to be no aid given out, and we were not to help these people in any way. These people were squatters on Government land, and the Government wanted them off it.* We were to do and give nothing that could possibly encourage them to stay there, including food, blankets and cooking utensils.

Now we faced a dilemma. We were in the country as guests of the Cambodian Government and had signed a contract agreeing to abide by the law. But we were also here in response to God's command to love and minister to the needs of the poor.

And these people had lost everything. This was the coolest part

123

of the year, and come nightfall they would be cold and hungry, with no shelter but the clothes they stood in.

With the rest of our team, we came together to pray and discuss our next step. As we thought about it, we realized that they had banned us from distributing aid on the fire site, but why couldn't we instead distribute aid to people at the community health clinic where we served the poor and sick a few kilometres south of the fire site? So that afternoon, with dozens of volunteers from local churches and youth groups, we went through the fire area, handing out vouchers to 900 families. On the voucher were directions to the Servants community clinic and the time that the emergency aid distribution would begin. Just to make sure nobody could get lost, we nailed bright yellow cardboard arrows to every fourth lamp post between the fire and distribution site.

The next day, volunteers from local churches worked alongside us as we distributed rice, bedding, mosquito nets, and cooking equipment to the families.

Because we were serving more than 6,000 people, we had to continue distribution the following morning. But about two hours into our second morning, we received a call that the Military Police had set up a road block just outside the fire area and were confiscating the emergency supplies from people as they tried to return to their burned out homes. Shocked, I jumped on a motorscooter with Pauv and sped back to Chbaa Ampou. Sure enough, just before the edge of the black ash and twisted metal, a dozen Military Police armed with AK 47's and several Government officials were fanned across the road. As each resident returned 'home' with their bundle of emergency supplies, they were stopped and their goods were seized.

Outraged, I strode towards the most important looking official in the group and demanded to know what he was doing, stealing food from the poor. He demanded to know why we were helping these squatters when the Government had said not to. I explained that I was with Servants, and we had an agreement with the Government to help the poor and needy in this area - and right now these were the neediest people around. Did he want them to starve? The work of Servants was well known in this district, and that brought us some credibility, but his orders from higher up over-rode that grudging respect.

Our argument rocked back and forth, neither of us willing to back down, as a Government official with a video camera insisted on filming the scene 'for the record,' and groups of residents observed us from a distance, and several officials made frantic calls on their cell phones, trying to get instructions about what they should do next with our rebellious little band.

Just when it seemed we were totally stale-mated, and that all of our careful planning was about to fail, a shiny blue car pulled up just short of the road block, and out stepped our friend, Rick Drummond, dressed in a dark blue suit and tie for a church service he was to lead later that morning. A tall, dignified man in his 60's, Rick was an elder statesman-missionary who had worked in Vietnam for many years before relocating to Cambodia, where he was now mentor and guide to an ethnic Vietnamese church in *Chbaa Ampou*, one of the churches participating with us in the emergency aid distribution effort. Rick had come down to check out how things were progressing.

The Government officials all looked up, slightly perturbed. *Who was this authoritative looking gentleman? Was he with me? Yes, I* replied, *he is an important American man who will be very angry when he sees what's going on here.* Their worried looks now became expressions of alarm. *You mean, this man is from the American Embassy? Well,* I replied, he *'belongs' to the American Embassy.* Rick certainly *was* an American citizen, I reasoned, and therefore under the authority and protection of the American Embassy.

I heard the soldiers in the background talking nervously, speculating that this new arrival was the American Ambassador. Suppressing a smile, I glanced in their direction and nodded. Quickly the rumour spread around the circle: this man in the suit was in fact the Ambassador of the United States of America! Rick, who was fluent in Vietnamese but didn't speak much Khmer, could see that he had become the center of attention and that his presence was causing quite a stir, but he had no idea why. "Kristin, what are they saying - what's going on?"

"I'll tell you later. Just look serious and keep nodding your head."

Quickly the group of Government officials withdrew into a huddle.

"OK, there's no big problem here," they told us. "We have decided to be generous and allow this aid to go through - everything except the tarpaulins." The tarpaulins, we were told, were a 'construction material' and would encourage these squatters to try and rebuild on the same site again.

The next day, after coming together with some of the other larger NGO's involved for a debriefing, we learned that some of these American-based NGO's had been asking their embassy to put pressure on the Cambodian Government over the way squatters were being treated, particularly regarding emergency aid. As a result, the aid embargo was completely lifted by the end of that day - and even tarpaulins were permitted.

Ironically, three days later, Servants received an official letter from the local Government office, thanking us for our years of cooperation and requesting us - if at all possible - to provide material aid to the 900 families who had so tragically lost their homes in the *Chbaa Ampou* fire.

In this heartbreaking situation, we—like so many others whose stories we have told here—were brought face to face with the injustice and inequity of a society that judges the rich to be worth more than the poor, and the powerful to have more rights than the already dispossessed.

In facing the conflict of interest between our commitment to respect the Cambodian Government and our commitment to serve the oppressed, we knew we had no other option but to side with the poor, for we serve a God who continually sides with the poor against their oppressors, and who demands that civil leaders protect their rights (e.g. Proverbs 31:8-9). This is what the prophets were doing when they denounced injustice meted out to the poor, and called Israel's rulers to account.

126

We also walk in the example of the disciples, who, when faced with a demand to back down from doing what Jesus had commanded them, retorted: "Whether it is right in the sight of God to listen to you more than to God, you judge. For we cannot but speak the things which we have seen and heard."[40] We in the West have amazing opportunities for education, health services, and acquiring wealth. Starvation no longer endangers us, but rather obesity - both physically and spiritually. But we did not receive these gifts so that we could spend them on ourselves, accumulating more and more, seeking greater and greater self-fulfillment.

Rather, we received these gifts for the good of others who have been starved of education, health, food, housing, sanitation, legal rights and daily necessities, so that we might enable them to find wholeness and fullness of life. In so doing, we allow more of God's Kingdom of righteousness and justice to come in this world.

If you have the financial means to buy this book, or the education that enables you to read it, you are one of the world's privileged citizens, one of its elite. And so live your life in the light of Jesus' challenge to his followers: "to those whom much has been given, of them much is expected." [41]

Let me be your hands and feet
Kristin Jack

Lord Jesus, come live in me by your Spirit
that I could embody and make real your love
in this weeping, broken world.
Let me become your hands, your flesh
reaching out beyond myself
to touch other people's pain and fear;
let me become your feet, your legs
sent to places of hurt and need
to speak good news and live your life
the life of love that makes my enemies my friends.
O Lord, let me put legs on your gospel
and be your hands and feet.
Give me your heart that I would feel what you feel,
give me your eyes that I would see what you see,
give me your mouth that I would speak your words,
give me your mind that I would do your will;
Come Lord Jesus, and live your life through me.

WHOLISM

1. Rene Padilla, Mission Between the Times, 22
2. Irenus, Bishop of Lyons (115-202), was mentored by Polycarp, who had been a disciple of the Apostle John.
3. John 15:12-14.
4. Matthew 5:43-48.
5. Luke 10:25-37.
6. Zechariah 14:20-21.
7. Revelation 21 & 22.
8. Gudrun Ahlers and Peter Sidebotham initiated this response to severe malnutrition in 1993.
9. Even in 2009, more than 40% of Cambodian children suffer from malnutrition (measured by the degree of wasting).
10. 2 Corinthians 10:3.
11. The Hebrew words sedeq/mishpat and the Greek words related to dikaiosune, translated as 'righteousness' in most of our English Bibles, are far more accurately represented by the couplet, 'righteousness and justice.' These are comprehensive words that embrace both inner morality and outer social justice.
12. As followers of Jesus, seeking to keep his teachings as faithfully as possible, Servants workers make an explicit commitment to peace-making and active non-violence (see Matthew 5:6-9, 5:38-48; Romans 12:9-21 for example). To read more about this theological position, see http://www.servantsasia.org/news.asp?number=182.
13. For the sake of security, the names of Servants workers in India have been altered.
14. idem. This story was written by Kristin Jack, based on an interview.
15. Sari Blankets are made by sewing together multiple layers of second-hand saris, which creates a beautiful quilting effect.
16. Both Sahara and Sharon continue today, and in fact have grown into two of the most respected Indian NGO's working in their areas.
17. TASK is a Khmer acronym for "Trotrung (ning) Akpiwat Sokapheap (neak) Kreykror," which in English translates, "Supporting the Health and Development of the Poor." While ministering in the slums of Phnom Penh, the Servants missionaries deliberately mentored and discipled their Khmer colleagues for more than ten years, passing on the health, educational, and spiritual resources they had benefited from in the West.
18. This was a common tactic used by the Khmer Rouge to destroy family bonds. Women were placed in one camp, men in another, and their children in yet another location. The children were then subjected to intense indoctrination and were often used as spies against their own parents, urged to report on any grumbling or signs of dissent. In this way children were often the instruments of their own parents' betrayal and death. The Khmer Rouge could allow no other loyalty except to the regime itself.
19. Eliana Hanni from Brazil worked with Sophat to help initiate this ministry in 1993.
20. The Khmer Rouge savagely persecuted the educated, the religious and the urban.
21. In particular, he worked on a huge port project that was supposed to extend a breakwater 3,000 meters into the sea north of Sihannoukville. But like most of the Khmer Rouge's ambitious projects, it was a failure and never completed (mostly because they had already executed all the nation's skilled engineers and technicians).
22. Those in that particular pagoda learned their medical skills from a doctor who had disguised himself as a monk and taken refuge there from the advancing Khmer Rouge. He was only able to do this for two months before he was discovered and executed.
23. Through the AIDS Home Care Programme, more than 800 people from urban poor communities have been regularly visited and ministered to with prayer, counselling, medicines and other practical help. Compassionate volunteers from those same communities (and their local churches) have been recruited and trained to help us do this visitation.
24. All meals were communal, since private property had been abolished.
25. The main form of public transport in Cambodia is a 90 or 110 cc motor scooter, which you hail and ride pillion for a negotiated price.
26. Jenny left Cambodia in the mid-1990s, and her administrative role - and the role of mentor to Pauv - was taken over by Alison Given.
27. For more information about TASK, go to www.task.org.kh; for Slumlight, e-mail slumlight@task.org.kh
28. Project HALO (Hope, Assistance, Love for Orphans) aims to keep orphaned children within

extended families and their communities wherever possible, sometimes recruiting Christian foster families or supporting teenager-headed households. Presently HALO supports over 600 orphans, ensuring that they are set in families, where they are loved, fed and kept in school.

29. This story was set before Anti-Retroviral Drugs (ARV's) became widely available in Cambodia (2006). Until then, HIV/AIDS was a death sentence, taking about eight months (on average) for the progression from initial illness to death. These days, TASK staff enable most patients to access ARV treatment.

30. This story was written by Kristin Jack, based on an interview.

31. The clinic provides HIV/AIDS education and medical treatment for sexually transmitted diseases. For every twelve cases of STDs treated, one case of AIDS is prevented, because STD's weaken (and sometimes ulcerate) the skin in the genital region. If you treat the STD, you can prevent HIV/AIDS. Through STD treatment and education about correct condom use, the spread of AIDS is being prevented. Through other education programs, men are being educated not to visit prostitutes.

32. All names in this story have been changed. Srey Neang is a common girls name and simply means 'girl' or 'woman.' Srey Kim Eng means 'young girl.' Srey Song Kim means 'girl of hope.'

33. This slum brothel was at the bottom end of the sex trade: less than a dollar a turn.

34. Servants' presence was tolerated in the brothel, but only to treat medical problems. These brothels were under the 'protection' of the local police, who congregated nearby, their pistols dangling conspicuously.

35. In Cambodia, illnesses are usually lumped together under a well known heading, such as 'fever,' or, as in this case, 'women's health problems.'

36. Cambodia has gained an ugly reputation as a haven for paedophiles and sex tourists, and there are brothels that exist especially to feed these predators. UNICEF estimates that globally, 1.2 million children are trafficked into prostitution every year (http://www.unicef.org/protection/index_exploitation.html). In the Philippines, there are 500,000 child prostitutes; in Cambodia, approximately half the prostitutes are minors; in India, a quarter of its 2.3 million prostitutes are underage, many smuggled in from Nepal and Bangladesh.

37. At this time, ECPAT was one of the few NGO's working in this kind of field, but even they had little experience at directly rescuing girls from brothels.

38. In Cambodia there is a repugnant saying: "men are like gold, women are like cloth." That is, if a man were to fall and become soiled, it's relatively easy for him to stand back up and wipe himself clean, but if a woman falls and loses her reputation, no matter how tragic the circumstances, she is a "srey kouch", a "ruined women" forever. In fact, "srey kouch" is the colloquial term for a prostitute.

39. The ministry that Rita helped initiate is still at work in this brothel, in partnership with White Lotus, a ministry devoted to helping women out of prostitution and providing a place of rehabilitation and vocational training.

40. Acts 4:20.

41. Luke 12:48b.

Four

SERVANTHOOD

*Give yourself fully to God. He will use you
to accomplish great things on the
condition that you believe much more in
His love than in your own weakness.*

Mother Teresa

INTRODUCTION: WAGING A WAR OF LOVE

Kristin Jack

*Your attitude should be the same as that of Jesus, who though being
in very nature God, did not consider this something to be clung to, but
emptying himself, he took on the nature of a servant.*

(Philippians 2:5-7)

*Now that I, your teacher and Lord have washed your feet, you
should do the same for one another. I have set you an example that you
should do as I have done for you. Now that you know these things,
how blessed you will be if you do them.*   (John 13:14, 15, 17)

We continually remember before our God and Father your work produced by faith, your labor prompted by love, and your endurance inspired by hope in our Lord Jesus Christ...Our gospel came to you not simply with words, but with power, and with the Holy Spirit and deep conviction. You know how we lived among you for your sake. You became imitators of us and of the Lord despite severe suffering, and you welcomed the message with the joy given by the Holy Spirit. And so you became a model to all the believers in the region.

(1 Thessalonians 1:2-7)

As Christians, we seek to follow the One who came in humility, 'not to be served, but to serve.'[1] As a mission, we demonstrate our commitment to this principle of servanthood by supporting local ministries that benefit the whole community, and by striving to raise up local leaders who will be agents of transformation in their neighborhoods. If love is our goal, we will set our hearts on meeting people's felt needs. Yet often the wisest thing missionaries or development workers can do 'for' the poor is to 'do' nothing at all, except to find out what God is already doing and join in. Rather than overpowering people with outside resources or expertise, we can choose to empower, encourage and support local people and local movements. Our real goal is to work 'with' the poor, not 'for' them.

In this section on servanthood, you will read stories about the forces of darkness bent on destroying people's lives, and about children who have suffered the pain of being abandoned in a concrete city of millions, knowing that nobody cares for them. You will also hear about street children whose lives have been changed by God's love and an AIDS patient who, though abandoned by his earthly family, died knowing that he was loved. As these stories demonstrate so beautifully, something good is happening, even in the face of overwhelming suffering, devastation and destruction. In all of these stories, we are seeking to live out the gospel of Christ's radical upside-down Kingdom: "Whoever among you wants to lead must become the servant of all the others."[2] And many times, as one Servants worker in India writes, as we meet Jesus among the poor, those we came to serve also serve us. At the end of the day, God would rather see us living in relationships of *mutual* servanthood (or friendship[3]) than charity or dependence.

The Christians you will read about here have sought to tap into the power of God's unyielding love and compassion, seeking to serve both neighbors and enemies. Challenging the forces of poverty and oppression will always bring us into conflict with the powers of darkness. Throughout the first three Gospels, there are numerous stories of Jesus confronting unclean or evil spirits to set people free from their enslavement. Sometimes these can only be dealt with by faith, prayer and fasting.

But Jesus also taught and demonstrated that spiritual warfare involves acts of love and works of service. The dark powers come to destroy; we come to heal. They come to sow hate and fear; we come to offer love and mercy. They come in rage; we come in peace. They come for revenge; we come to forgive. They come to dominate and manipulate; we come to empower and serve. They come to curse; we come to bless. They come to take; we come to give. We come in the opposite spirit.

As Paul put it, we do not wage war the way the world does, but rather, "Bless those who curse you...do not repay anyone evil for evil...do not take revenge but leave that to God...on the contrary: if your enemy is hungry, feed him; if he is thirsty, give him something to eat...do not be overcome with evil, but overcome evil with goodness." [5] No, we do not wage war as the world does. Instead we wage peace and love in the Way of our Servant-King.

The Witch Doctor's Death

Craig Greenfield

(Phnom Penh, Cambodia)

Craig Greenfield is the International Coordinator of Servants. Though he wrote this article while living in Phnom Penh, working with children orphaned by HIV/AIDS, he and his wife, Nayhouy, and their two children, Jayden and Micah, have since relocated to Vancouver, Canada, in order to begin a community working with the inner-city poor there.

The week we set up our first home in the Stung Mein Chey slum, one of our first visitors was the local witch doctor. He had come to see whether we would pay him some money to pray a blessing on our home. We gently told him that we had already asked Jesus to bless and protect our home.

As we sat around in a circle on the floor of our new house, sipping water, he suddenly took a noisy suck and then sprayed it over one corner of the room. Another big suck and then WHOOOOSH, he sprayed the water over another corner of the room. Then came muttering and whispering. Nayhouy and I looked at each other incredulously and shook our heads in disbelief. He was giving us a freebie!

The next day, our Cambodian friends told us that his ritual was quite normal and might have been a blessing or a curse—only the witch doctor would know.

Needless to say, we spent some extra time praying through our house that day!

As the years unfolded we got to know the witch doctor and his family, as they lived just two doors down. His first son had contracted dengue fever and died within days. His other son was born with Downs Syndrome and suffered merciless teasing from the other kids in the village. We got to know him fairly well, because he loved to come and play with the toys at our house.

A couple of years later, as the witch doctor lay dying of cancer,

134

we were drawn into his home. Unpopular in the community, he had no visitors and his wife struggled to care for him alone. We visited most days, bringing soya milk—the only thing he could stomach. His cancer of the throat and mouth had left him barely able to swallow, and a huge pus-filled wound had to be cleaned daily. As I watched his faithful wife pour water into his parched mouth, the water dripped out a gaping cancerous hole under his chin. The stench was almost unbearable. As we sat by his bedside, he agreed that we could pray for him, and we shared from our heart about Jesus many times.

Finally he died, and though we did not know whether he was at peace with God since he was unable to speak those last days—we knew that God allowed us to be a part of his suffering for a reason.

Soon after he died, half of our community was evicted to make way for a new Government sewer system. We moved out of that slum and into another and lost contact with the witch doctor's widow. But on a visit to our community, after more than two years away, I decided to visit her.

As I nudged open the door to her small wooden home and my eyes adjusted to the dim lighting, I saw sitting on the floor a circle of perhaps ten or fifteen men and women, each with an open Bible, worshipping God. As the widow looked up at me, I could see by her face that her life had been transformed. The story spilled out of how she had decided to become a follower of Jesus and how God was blessing her family, who were all now believers.

I was stunned to learn that each week a small group of believers met as a house church in the witch doctor's home. Our attempts to obey God and serve those around us often seem so small and feeble. But we offer them with faith, love, and hope—for we never know what God is going to do with them.

Shabu's Children[6]

Daniel Wartenweiler

(Manila, Philippines)

Daniel Wartenweiler arrived in Manila from Switzerland in the late 1990s. Deeply moved by the desperate plight of those living on Manila's streets, particularly the children, he began a ministry called Bulilet, which means 'little one.' The vision of Bulilet, similar to Onesimo,[7] is to see the lives of Manila's street children changed by God's love as they come into contact with staff on the streets, at the drop-in centre, in the residential therapeutic communities, or through God's creation at Camp Rock. Daniel is partnered in this ministry by his wife, Lynette, who is a gifted Social Worker.

Rowena

In one of the poorest, densest parts of Metro Manila, beneath the darkness cast by a hulking concrete fly-over for traffic crossing the Pasig River, inside a tiny cubicle of cardboard, plywood and plastic lives six-year-old Rowena, the second youngest of six siblings. In this settlement of around 150 families and 500 children, there are no toilets, no running water - besides the stinking, foul river that oozes behind the settlement - no ventilation and no legal electricity. A thick, black mud lines the narrow alleys, and the air is a sour mixture of sweat, urine, rats and garbage.

Rowena's 'neighborhood' is a centre for drugs, gambling and violence. Like the other children who live here, she has been trained how to deal shabu because she is quick and not likely to be suspected by the authorities. With her mother in jail, she takes orders from her father or other dealers in the settlement, running drugs to customers by hiding it in her clothes. Though the money from running shabu might bring a minimum daily wage, most everything is taken by her father - and if she doesn't make enough, she will be beaten.

Rowena's eyes glint with a mixture of fear and anger, knowing she can trust no-one. Her ten-year-old sister, Angie, has already been sent to the Government's "reception and action centre", and fourteen-year-old Abigail is serving time in a women's jail, where she is 'educated' by the adult prisoners. What will become of this wild little girl, who is unable to respect authority? Will she ever escape this spiral of drugs, violence and poverty? Will she, like so many others, be rounded up by the police, the victim of a street 'clean-up' campaign, a frightening raid where streetkids are trucked off to distant institutions?

Jessica

When I first started working with kids like Rowena and Jessica, my Tagalog language was still limited and broken, as I had arrived in the neighboring squatter area only eight months earlier. Moved by the changed lives I was seeing in the therapeutic communities of Onesimo, I decided I wanted to spend more time out on the streets reaching others who also needed that opportunity. There, I was deeply touched and shaken by the pain and loneliness of so many children, many as young as Jessica, who roamed the streets rather than return to broken and abusive homes. I spent many evenings out on the streets, always going back to the same places. I wanted to know more about the lives of these kids. I wanted to be their friend, to spend time running, playing, telling stories and just listening to them.

From across the street, Jessica recognises me and runs straight into my arms. Once again I'm dazzled by her smile and her huge dark eyes. She wants to be picked up and hugged, but then she pulls my hair and slaps my face to get down. Unable to be still for more than a few seconds, she sprints across the paved area in front of the big Catholic Cathedral, the 'playground' for the children of Quiapo, a bustling rundown neighborhood in central Manila. Running up behind some older kids, she thumps them on the back and kicks at their backsides to get attention. They turn and hit her until she falls to the pavement, crying. Then she's up and running again, trying to get my attention by whacking me or throwing something at me. I pick her up in my arms, knowing she is starving for attention, care and love, like so many of the other children who roam the streets rather than return to violent homes. Jessica is one of the youngest kids in the group, and she has developed her own strategy for survival. She is fast and aggressive, almost violent. But because of her eccentric behaviour she is frequently getting beaten-up by older kids. Neglected and often without the care of a loving parent, all these children survive by begging, selling little flowers, or stealing, sleeping with friends and siblings on pieces of cardboard along the paved sidewalks. If they get sick, nobody cares. If they get lost, sold or taken by the police, nobody notices. I wait for Jessica to become quiet, to rest in the safety I hope to offer.

When I first met Jessica, she was a little four-year-old girl dressed in a T-shirt rag so big that it fell below her knees. Her bare feet were black from dirt and soot. Her hands and legs were covered with scars and dirty, infected sores. Her face was filthy, but her eyes were alive and sparkling. Jessica's mother took shabu daily during her pregnancy, which helps explain Jessica's attention deficit problems, and she is now in jail for dealing drugs. Like her father, who is an addict, Jessica and her three older siblings live on the streets, looking after themselves.

When our team opened a small shelter for the kids from Quiapo, Jessica threw herself into my arms, crying: "Nobody is feeding me – nobody cares about me. Please take me with you to the center." After getting her father's agreement, she was the second child to come and live in our therapeutic community. A very physical, wild child, Jessica often loses control, but over the course of two years, we began to see significant progress.

Then her mother was released from jail, and Jessica was attracted to the streets again. After running away from the centre several times, she left to live with her mother and father in a small shanty they'd rented under the bridge. Her parents are still taking drugs, and all four of the siblings are dealing shabu in the slum. Jessica roams the streets day and night without supervision, occasionally returning to her parents' home, where she is often beaten by her father.

But Jessica still shows up at the center, asking for a shower, a meal, or a hug. We don't know what the future holds for Jessica, but we will not give up. We will keep sharing God's love, hoping and praying for her, and our door will always be open anytime she wants to come back.

Nika

Slumped on the pavement of the Manila street that doubles as her home, eight year old Nika looked like a ghost. Her face, stomach, arms and legs were covered with toothpaste[8] to "cool" the burns covering her body. Big blisters were festering under a hard crust of dry toothpaste. Desperate to protect her two-year-old brother, Joshua, from the flames of a methane gas explosion that had ripped through the garbage where they were scavenging, Nika had used her own body as a shield.

Nika's mother and father, both shabu addicts, were in jail. Her four year old sister had disappeared. After badgering Nika's aunt until she promised to bring her niece to a clinic the following day, we gathered to pray around Nika: *'Lord Jesus, please heal Nika and don't let her die.'*

But for the next two days, I couldn't find Nika anywhere. When I finally found her begging on the streets, I could see that one big blister covering her entire tummy had burst and was filled with black grime. Bundling Nika up in my arms, I rushed her to the hospital, where I had to beg the staff to admit the dirty little girl in my arms into their nice clean rooms. I talked two teenage street girls, dressed in threadbare clothes, into staying with Nika, as no nursing care was provided, and they found the courage and kindness to stay in that cold environment of crisp white uniforms and unwelcoming stares.

Four days later, Nika was ready to be discharged, but there was no way that she could go back onto the streets, for she had been heavily wrapped in bandages. After staying for a few days in the girl's home run by Onesimo, we found a Christian community to care for her and Joshua. In that Christian community, Nika's wounds have been healing both inside and out as she and her brother have come to know the love of 'the Father of the fatherless.' Though a few scars remain across her stomach, her long, dark hair is full again, and her face is filled with joy.

God's Children

After a while other young people from the Onesimo therapeutic communities, whose lives were changing for the better, started joining me on the streets. The vision was taking hold amongst those who themselves had been helped, and a team formed which regularly went out to minister to these abandoned children. We were able to take some of the kids on their first ever holiday to Camp Rock, located on a beautiful golden beach. This was their first respite ever from the years of fighting to survive on the streets. None of them had ever dreamed that such a beautiful place even existed in their own country. They had never swum anywhere but the filthy Pasig River, which runs through Metro Manila. They had never built a sand castle or climbed over big salt-stained rocks. They had never smelt the fresh breeze coming from the sea, nor heard a bird singing, nor been surrounded by lush green nature. All they knew was the concrete of the streets, the noise of the traffic and the smell of pollution. And most of them had never felt loved and had never experienced the security of a family or the stability of a home.

As we gathered one night on the beach around a big wooden cross, every child was given a stone to symbolize the heaviness of their lives. We invited the children to come to the cross with their stones and lay them down there. For a few moments it was totally quiet, apart from the distant sound of waves rhythmically washing the shore. Then the first child stood up and brought his stone to the cross. In the minutes that followed, every child - from the youngest four-year-old boy to the oldest fifteen-year-old girl - came to the cross, bearing a stone. They knelt down in the sand, their tear-stained faces glistening in the candlelight. One child began to weep with great sighs, then another, and another. For more than an hour, we knelt with the children in front of the cross, holding them and praying for them, amazed by how God had melted their hearts. These children were no longer shabu's children, but had been adopted into the family of God. Like the nearby surf caressing the beach, these precious children were being healed by wave after wave of Christ's love.

A Lighthouse In A Sea Of Poverty

Rachel Hauser

(Manila, Philippines)

Rachel Hauser arrived in Manila from Switzerland in 1990. In that time she has been a friend and mentor to many. She helps lead 'Lilok', a learning community that uses informal educational approaches to prepare pastors and other community leaders (such as Ruth in this story) for ministry among the poor. Rachel is also presently working to create a clean, green, eco-friendly retreat site for the urban poor just outside of Manila.

Just behind the international harbour on Manila Bay lies the old city district of Tondo, one of the most over-crowded municipalities in the world's most densely populated city.[9] Teeming with some of the poorest neighborhoods among Manila's jostling millions, many temporary housing compounds in Tondo were erected in the mid-1990s after the Philippine Government forcibly closed "Smokey Mountain," the garbage dump where thousands had lived and worked for many years. [10] These temporary housing compounds consist of huge two-story warehouse sheds, subdivided with thin plywood walls into units of twelve square meters. Each unit houses one or two families with multiple family members - seven or eight children, grandparents, uncles and aunts. For every two units, there is one tiny bathroom equipped with a tap and a squat toilet. Natural light and ventilation are poor. But the corridor between the rows of units bustles with life, as children and adults revel in this precious 'open' space.

During the Smokey Mountain struggle, Ruth Palma emerged as a fierce community organizer and advocate for her people's land and rights. The wife of a local pastor and a teacher by training, Ruth also moved to Tondo and became burdened by the children drifting aimlessly around the housing compounds. Without school and basic literacy, these children faced a future as despairing and impoverished as their parents, or perhaps worse. Very likely they would slip into street life - their petty crime leading to violent crime, their hopelessness leading to drugs and alcohol, their lack of belonging pointing them toward eventual gang membership.

In response, Ruth opened the *'Lighthouse Preschool'* in the corridor of one of the compound's halls. With roughly 160 pupils on its roll, the preschool offers surprisingly orderly classes amidst the activity swirling around it. Knowing that the students' physical and mental development will not improve without adequate nutrition, the preschool also offers a simple lunch each day. With a charismatic personality and a heart for those trapped in poverty and suffering all around her Ate (aunty) Ruth is constantly exploring new ways to improve conditions, and because of her obvious love for her community, she quickly gains their trust. But more children want to come to the Lighthouse than there is space available, and because so few families in the area earn more than a subsistence income, parents cannot pay tuition. Thus keeping the school open is an ongoing struggle.

On one of the days when I visit the Lighthouse, the class is already in full swing. Ruth is teaching the fifty-some students in her class by microphone to overcome the background noise swirling through the housing complex. Yet the pupils are focused and listening intently as she leads them through song and craft.

But the school has run out of money, and so there will be no lunch. Then a small miracle occurs: someone in this poor community has supplied the school with cake for today—one piece for each child! Surprised and joyful, every teacher and student offers up thanks to the God of the universe, the One who promises to supply all that we need. I notice that one small boy is not eating his cake, but keeping it carefully wrapped. When I ask him if he isn't hungry, he explains that his mother is at home sick, and that there is no food in the house. Since she is unable to work, he would rather go hungry so that she might eat and get her strength back.

After school is over, Ruth takes us with her to visit some of the families in the community. Most of the mothers we meet look tired and pale – not surprising given their cramped, dim houses, poor diets and heavy workloads. But Ruth has a genuine gift for putting people at ease, able to find common ground with each person we visit. As we move about the community, children's faces light up when they realize that Ate Ruth is coming to visit, and I am struck by the shining eyes and healthy hair, as well as the glimpses of hope and self-confidence, among the children who attend the Lighthouse.

On a tenement rooftop we find Jun-Rey and Philip, ages six and eight, who have dropped out of the Lighthouse school to scavenge. As they search the streets and garbage-dump for cans, glass, plastic, and cardboard to sell to recyclers, they risk exposure to disease, cuts from sharp debris, and death from the bulldozers that work the garbage heaps. Their clothes are stained black, and they reek of glue. [11] With downcast eyes, drained of light and hope, they haltingly tell us their decision to stop coming to the school so that they can earn a few more cents for their families each day.

After descending the stairs from the rooftop, we visit the unit where the boy who didn't eat his cake lives. Like so many of the women in Tondo, his mother looks tired and drained. "This will be my breakfast," she tells us, holding up the cake. She is too embarrassed to say it more plainly: there is no other food in the house. Moved, we praise her son, affirming his deep love and care for her.

Later, after discussing how we might help this family in a way that will not rob them of dignity but bring them strength, we bow our heads and pray that the Lighthouse will keep shining, offering an alternative future for the children of Tondo. There is pain and poverty here. But there is also light.

Beyond The Stare

Les McCrostie

(Bangkok, Thailand)

Les McCrostie arrived in Bangkok from New Zealand in the early 1990s, where she served for several years. Along with her Servants teammates, she helped establish House of Life, a discipleship home for young Thais coming out of drug addiction. As the AIDS epidemic spread through Thailand in the 1990s, the House of Life team found themselves loving and nursing their dying friends instead.[12]

Sitting in the Bangkok public hospital, I looked around at the sunken eyes, taut, yellow skin and skeletal frames of the abandoned bodies surrounding me. This impersonal ward had become a human waste heap, a dumping ground for these men between the ages of nineteen and forty who were dying of AIDS.[13] I knew that by next week, many of these men would be gone, and there would be a whole new set of lonely faces.

Bick, the young man I was caring for, was incontinent, dehydrated and exhausted. His body had been battling symptoms for months, and he didn't have much fight left. We had rung his mother to tell her that Bick was dying, but she had told us that she was 'tied up with business', meaning she was busy gambling and playing card games in her slum.

"I can't do this by myself," I thought as I washed Bick, straining to turn and lift him alone. Sandy, my teammate, who usually visited the hospital with me, was back in Australia. I was exhausted physically, but also emotionally as I looked around at the weeping sores and pleading eyes of so many who were suffering.

After washing and powdering Bick, I massaged and exercised the wasted muscles in his emaciated legs. "Thank you," he whispered, sitting up in his bed, which I had made with fresh sheets. His thin lips stretched into a wide smile and his big dark eyes twinkled.

Bick knew that his death was imminent, but he had recently

encountered Jesus. Though his body was wracked with pain, I felt deep reassurance knowing that Bick saw himself as a child of God, and knew he was loved unconditionally.

I glanced up and saw a Thai woman staring at me. As the seconds passed, I felt as though I could read her thoughts: *"What is this foreigner doing here? Why is she washing and caring for this young Thai man? This can't be right – you just don't see foreigners here – not helping on the wards of one of our hospitals!"*

She leaned over the pale, listless body of a teenager, her face full of bewilderment and pain.

As our eyes met and locked, I knew that the boy was her son, and I thought of all the love with which she had nurtured him over the years, the dreams she had treasured for her little boy - all snatched away by an aching grief as she watched him slowly die.

Reaching over, I took her hand in mine, and my eyes welled up with tears. Here was one woman whose love for her son outweighed the shame, gossip and fear of contagion that no doubt isolated her from her neighbors. But she had gained a special bond with her son that Bick's mother would never know about. Though we were strangers, and spoke each other's language imperfectly, I knew as we grasped hands that we understood one another and why we were here, sharing this road of suffering.

She released my grip and gently brushed her boy's hair, as I imagined she had done countless times when he was little. His eyes drifted open, and a smile broke across his pinched face, softening his sunken features. Like Bick, he too knew he was loved.

She Loved

David Boone

(India/USA)

David was raised in Europe and attended Wheaton College, where he experienced urban outreach and a desire to serve among the poor. After completing his electrical engineering degree at the University of Maryland, he moved to Chicago and married Amy Jo, where they served the needs of the poor community through a local church. They moved to India with Servants in early 1998, where they lived until his daughter's birth and Amy Jo's death at the end of 1999.

I found myself being swept along in the midst of a funeral procession, surrounded by young men from the Baghel Thakur clan. How could this be?

My wife Amy Jo and I had moved into Shri Niwas Puri area nearly two years earlier, eager to live intentionally among the poor. We wanted to make friends, to share their lives, to hear their stories, to serve them, and to communicate the good news of Jesus Christ.

Now as I sat in the lead car of the 'akhira yatra', the final journey, I felt a deep, sad kinship with my neighbors.

I remembered back to the sweltering summer day when Dev Lal had approached me. "Friend," he said, "follow me". I followed him down our narrow alley to the little community temple, hoping we wouldn't be going too far, me dressed in my wrap around lungi and all. Beyond the temple courtyard was a musty room, furnished with a half-dozen charpai rope beds and a couple of ceiling fans; young men lounging about, napping, shooting the breeze; khadi-clad elders gathered around the hookah. I was offered a toke on the pipe and a drink from the local well. A few days earlier I had expressed my loneliness to a shopkeeper. Word got around, and the guys had decided to extend their friendship. I was invited to come back as often as I liked. And I had. Often I would listen to the elders discuss the local gossip, negotiate community conflicts, and sometimes debate religious questions. I'd write down words I didn't understand to look up later.

I was welcomed into a type of community that I had never experienced before.

While no one (except for untold numbers of children and our landlady) ever felt comfortable dropping in on us, it was expected that I walk into their homes without knocking, whereupon I could expect to be offered a meal. Often I would go watch TV with Netram, or hang out at the ice cream cart with Vinod. Slowly I was able to enter their world and see life from their perspective. Later, I was the guest of honor at Netram's wedding, and indeed, I felt honored.

My wife, Amy Jo spent most of her time in the neighborhood. Her gentle spirit and sincere affection for people attracted the women and children. She immediately established a friendship with our landlady, Malti. Malti's children Babita, Mumta, and Bala were the first to come see the strange foreigners. Then boisterous Puja and shy Punit. I learned my Hindi colors from games of UNO with these kids. Soon it was Anu, Nitu and Sonia, and then the girls from across the gully. It was all a bit overwhelming for me; I wanted more time alone, to think, to process. Amy Jo was welcoming the kids, and I was sending them away. Her heart came alive when she could shower affection on the children whose parents were busy struggling to make ends meet. So Amy Jo would color with the kids, and I'd be on the roof with my journal.

Amy Jo taught arts and crafts in a program for kids whose parents depended on them for their livelihoods. They were mostly Bangledeshi migrants and Muslim, despised by our "less" poor neighbors. She willingly rubbed shoulders with the unlovely, pausing to hug a begging woman, to place the coin in the hands of a leper, to carry a dirty child. One boy in our neighborhood would constantly show off, seeking our attention. I couldn't suppress a dislike for his antics, but Amy Jo would praise him for his dancing and encourage his singing. He moved later, when his mother died, but he would travel far to see "Auntie", who reserved a special compassion for him.

Amy Jo and I seized every opportunity to deepen our relationships and to experience our neighbor's lives. We sat in the shade and sweated with them during power outages. We slept with Malti's family on the roof. We went with Malti and her family to nearby dramas and festivals. We traveled together to Malti's village for a weekend. Together we celebrated holidays, weddings, and births. And yes, there were also deaths.

Now, in the funeral procession, the akhira yatra, I couldn't help but think how this might yet again strengthen our ties, open hearts, allow the hope of the gospel to be communicated. I wanted to know what they thought about the afterlife, what their customs were, how they coped with death. I had seen the grace and resilience of India's poor as they bore suffering after suffering, and I wanted to know it too.

A young woman, Asha, had died unexpectedly, suddenly, leaving her husband with a newborn girl.

I had witnessed it all, watched the community respond. The news traveled quickly, and people gathered to hear the details, to see the baby, to lay hands of condolence on the husband, still in shock.

Asha had enjoyed a healthy pregnancy and the community was sharing her joy. Then, in her eighth month of pregnancy, she developed severe headaches. She was treated at the nearest hospital, where few of her poorer neighbors could have gained access. Her friends were concerned, and prayed to their gods: Sai Baba, Mata Di, Shri Krishna. Somewhat unusual for this neighborhood, Asha was Isai, a follower of Jesus. Her family prayed fervently for Jesus to heal her. Her child was delivered premature – a girl. Urgent, emergency surgery was needed to remove the fast growing tumour from her brain. She briefly survived the surgery, waking long enough to touch her daughter, but then falling back into unconsciousness and within a few hours, dying.

When the new father returned from the hospital with the news, there was a gasp of unbelief. She had been so healthy, just days before. News spread quickly, and before long the room was crowded with people, laying their hands on him in silent condolence.

There was sorrow, and there was joy. There was death, and there was life. Asha (meaning hope) had died, and Kiran (meaning sunshine) had been born.

Arrangements were quickly made for the funeral. "Would she be cremated?" they wondered. What do Isai people do? When they found out about the burial customs, the elders protested. They wanted a viewing in the community. They eventually settled on accompanying her body from the hospital to the cemetery for a viewing there. The journey was the key thing. A chance to send her off. A chance to say goodbye.

One devout young man urged everyone to come; Asha, in a dream, had come to him and implored them all to be there. A collection was made to rent a bus, no small thing for these struggling, working-class people. I was compelled by my friends to travel with them in a car at the front of the procession; we were followed by the bus and the ambulance, bearing the casket. I sat arm in arm with them, respectfully silent, absorbed in thought.

And then we entered the cemetery, where each person took a final look; some sprinkled flower petals on the woman's body. Asha's grief-stricken parents followed in turn, her mother pausing to weep. I too took a final look, but my eyes did not linger. A glance was enough to see that her soul had departed, leaving only a lifeless shell. I wanted to cry, but I could not. I was numb, in shock. Because this experience, shared as it was with my neighbors, was more personal still. The widower was me, the baby girl was mine, and lying in the casket was "Asha", Amy Jo, my wife.

I looked around at those who shared my grief. American friends and family, Australian and Kiwi team mates, Christian brothers and sisters from the four corners of India. And the Hindi-speaking neighbors we had come to serve. Thirty women or so. Malti, our landlady, a widow herself. Jayanti, Om Prakash's wife. Om Butti. I walked over to sit with the men: the elders of the community; Netram, whose wedding I had attended; Krishn, Malti's son; Dev Lal's father, also a widower.

I had never experienced such quiet in India before. I could hear the wind chasing the birds through the trees. In Shri Niwas Puri, where

200 families occupied a single block, there were always the shouts of children, the vegetable seller, the cry of a baby, the temple music, the call to prayer. But here, in a sacred moment, there was silence.

Kiran and I moved back into Shri Niwas Puri a few weeks later, with daily visits from my team mates. I wasn't expected to stay, but this was home. I wasn't ready to leave. But nothing really went right in those weeks. I was fighting both American expectations and Indian traditions. I was fighting myself. Yet the loss was so deep, the hurt so acute, I couldn't bring myself to let go just yet: to relinquish the dreams we had dreamt, the relationships we had nurtured, the identity we had chosen. And sticking it out had other benefits: hearing about the love my neighbors had for Amy Jo, and receiving consolation from them.

My neighbors knew Asha, the person Amy Jo had become. They were able to share memories that few back home would relate too. As I listened to them, I heard the sadness, the unbelief, the loss of one they had loved. They praised Asha, who had been so loving with the neighborhood kids. "God knew she would never get to love her own," they said. Malti was close to Amy Jo. In many ways they were kindred spirits. Like Amy Jo, she exuded peace and gentleness. She was poor, but lived her life with joy. At Asha's memorial service, Malti eulogized:

"Asha was like a member of our family. She loved us a lot. We went so many places together with Amy Jo. We used to share meals. We thought a lot of her. She loved us so very much!"

There is no doubt that consolation was meaningful coming from those who had been through deep loss. Hindi, like English, has its trite proverbs at the ready. "What God does is good," was tossed at me more than once. But most of my neighbors had experienced heart-wrenching deaths of at least one family member, something less common in the States.

In the coming weeks Malti would share her story with me. Her husband had been a drinker and gambler, and when he died in an auto-rickshaw accident, she was left with four young children and nearly broke. Her father-in-law allowed Malti to stay on his son's property, but he didn't give a single penny towards his grandchildren's needs. She was forced to abandon her children during the day to make a pitiful wage in a factory. She told me how much better things are now, but how, sometimes, when no one is looking, she still bears her grief in tears. I wondered if I would be able to bear my tragedy as gracefully as she. It was from Malti, more than anyone else, that I gathered hope. And it is hope by which we, the broken, endure.

Amy Jo (Asha) was raised in Pakistan with her siblings Jim and Laura, where her parents ministered to the Christian community through seminary training. She immensely enjoyed her schooling at Murree Christian School, with kids from all over the world. Her experiences at Wheaton College, particularly an internship in Thailand through the HNGR program, gave her a deep awareness of third world poverty and aroused in her a longing to serve among the poor.

David was raised in Europe where his father served in the U.S. Air Force. He also attended Wheaton College where he first experienced urban outreach and a desire to serve among the poor. David completed his electrical engineering degree at the University of Maryland and moved to Chicago to work in his field while living simply among the poor.

David and Amy Jo met and began their marriage in Uptown, an inner city neighborhood of Chicago, where they served the needs of the community through a local church. They made their first trip to India together in 1996 where they were happily recruited by Servants. They moved to India in early 1998, where they lived until Kiran's birth and Amy Jo's death at the end of 1999.

David returned to Chicago in 2000, where he took up software design part-time while enjoying a special relationship with his daughter, Kiran. God again gave David the gift of a partner - and Kiran the gift of a new mother - when he was joined in marriage with Hyacinth Rajadurai in 2006.

She loved

She loved green.
Green glass.
Her eyes.
She loved blue. And white.
The color of flat-roofed houses
dotting the Greek islands.
My eyes.

She loved peace.
Born in Pindi. Died in Delhi.
She wished they could make up.

She loved sunflowers.
Like the ones in Colorado near the
train tracks and the red clay road.

She loved mountains. Beaches.
And Romance.

She loved to be simple.
In heart. In mind.
She loved beauty.
Beauty and simplicity.
Painted flower pots.

She loved.

D.B.

Fleeing Cambodia

Craig and Nayhouy Greenfield

Nayhouy, along with her mother and brother, fled Cambodia as a six-year-old. She experienced growing up as a refugee in New Zealand, but always knew that God would one day call her back to her homeland to minister to her people.

Nayhouy was born towards the end of 1973, as Khmer Rouge forces began to put a strangle hold on her home town of Battambang, in the northwest of Cambodia. Nayhouy was not yet two when the Khmer Rouge took Phnom Penh, marking the end of a protracted civil war and ushering in a four-year nightmare that would stretch to two decades without resolution.

Within the space of a few weeks, after the fall of the capital city, all the urban centers across the country had been evacuated and the entire population was forced to work the fields. One early morning in April, 1975, a crude band of Khmer Rouge soldiers marched into her provincial town and down the main street. Nayhouy was playing happily outside, oblivious to the turmoil, and her mother - pregnant with Nayhouy's brother - was still optimistic that the end of the civil war would mean peace and the return of her husband, who was a Government police officer.

A few weeks later, three trucks jammed with people rumbled slowly by. Khmer Rouge soldiers trooped alongside the swaying vehicles, their leaders calling over loudspeakers for more townspeople to come forward and climb on the trucks, "Comrades, all those who are highly educated and all who have experience in the previous administration are urgently needed to help rebuild the country." The trucks rumbled on, not turning off towards the town square or City Hall, but straight out of town and into the jungle. When nobody saw those passengers again, Nayhouy's mother and their neighbors grasped the full horror of the darkness descending upon Cambodia.

Over the next months and years Nayhouy heeded her mother's

warning to say nothing of their background or identity. Nayhouy's father had been fighting against the Khmer Rouge for several years as a military policeman on the side of the Government, trying to keep the communists from taking over the capital city. It had been six months since they had last seen him. One afternoon, Nayhouy watched her mother spend hours removing any trace of their Government connections from the simple wooden home they shared with her grandfather and other relatives.

Soon the townspeople had all been ordered by the new regime to leave their homes in the city and build thatch shelters alongside the fields where they were to work.

Long days turned to long months, and Nayhouy's father never returned. He had disappeared without a trace, one of the thousands of Khmer Rouge victims whose bodies were never identified. Her father never knew the baby son who was born to him late one Saturday night under the thatch roof of a temporary shelter. Her mother's muffled screams and birth pains were attended to by Nayhouy's bustling aunties, with a wizened traditional birth attendant finally arriving about half an hour after the boy gasped his first breath.

With two young children to care for and no husband to help, food was scarce and Nayhouy's mother began to watch the effects of hunger strip the life from their once healthy bodies. One sweltering, humid lunchtime, after days with nothing to eat but watery rice soup, Nayhouy and her tiny brother lay lethargic on the floor of their hut. The children's eyes were dull and their skin dry and loose with malnutrition. Nayhouy watched her mother kneel in tears and whisper a prayer on behalf of her children. Then her mother lay face down on the bamboo floor of the hut as if waiting to die, gazing with watery eyes through the slats at the dirty brown seasonal flood waters that were beginning to rise below her tiny home. Suddenly, Nayhouy's mother jumped to her feet and called in excitement to Nayhouy's aunt, Yary, to bring a stick.

Though it was strictly forbidden to catch anything for personal consumption, Nayhouy watched her mother and aunt splashing through the water and, suppressing hysterical laughter, whacking at the fish in the shallow flood waters below the hut. Nayhouy watched in glee as victorious, the two women yanked fish after fish out of the water, beaming at their prize. That night they all feasted on the timely catch and thanked God again for sparing the lives of the children.

The months continued to pass in a monotony of toil and quiet desperation. Nayhouy's mother was forced to return to work in the fields soon after the birth, while Nayhouy herself had to spend the day looking after her little brother. At four, Nayhouy was really too young for such responsibility and it's a wonder that either of the children survived the flood waters and other dangers that swirled around them.

Each night Nayhouy would massage her mother's blistered feet in an attempt to bring her some comfort. Actually, her mother had never worked in a field before: her parents had been merchants (noodle sellers), city people. No one in the whole family had ever been rice farmers. But young as she was, Nayhouy had to promise her mother she would never divulge that information to anyone. The Khmer Rouge ideology was to make Kampuchea into one vast farm manned by unquestioning peasants toiling like ants from dawn to dusk. In such a 'utopia', there was no room for merchants, business people, teachers, doctors, nurses or 'intellectuals'. They had soft hands and questioning minds, and the regime had no use for them, other than to use their bodies to fertilize their insatiable rice fields. Cambodia had been transformed into a country-wide gulag, slave camp, killing field. Nayhouy dared not ask about her father and what had become of him. Without the aid of photos or any other memento, she struggled to even recall what he looked like.

One day, Nayhouy watched as one of the Khmer Rouge soldiers guarding their camp slowed to watch her mother clumsily swinging her bamboo hoe. With the end of his weapon he prodded her roughly: "show me your hands." Nayhouy's mother reluctantly turned her palms up. Though now blistered and grimy, they were clearly the soft hands of someone who was not used to manual labor. Narrowing his eyes, he snarled, "Comrade, if you are truly who you claim to be, you will certainly be able to plant this whole field with potatoes by the end of the day. By yourself!" He motioned to a large empty field nearby.

Nayhouy's mother turned her head quickly to glance at the daunting field, then lowered her eyes and murmured assent. The soldier made himself comfortable alongside two others beneath the scant shade of some nearby trees, and waited to see how Nayhouy's mother would respond.

Swinging her bamboo hoe in an arc above her head, Nayhouy's mother let it fall heavily on the sun-baked dirt, chipping away a hole where later she would place a small potato plant. Hour after hour she laboured, intent on her task, only looking up occasionally to make sure Nayhouy and her brother were still safe at the edge of the field. Finally, late in the afternoon, aching and fatigued, she planted the last potato seedling in its hole. The soldiers were mollified for the time being and allowed them to limp back to their sleeping mat for what remained of the night.

The next day however, the soldiers were back, motioning to an even larger field. Her mother's hands were badly blistered from the previous day's labor, but she knew she had no choice. Once again she clenched her teeth and gripped her hoe with determination, trying to ignore the pain in her back and her weeping hands. Once more, by some miracle of will-power and unknown grace, by the end of the day she had again finished planting the field. They stumbled home humiliated and exhausted, Nayhouy's mother dragging the blood-stained hoe along the ground.

On the third day, the soldiers were no longer laughing. Churlishly, they indicated a much larger area, twice the size of the field she had planted on the first day. Nayhouy's mother once more wound her palms around the hoe, wincing with pain. Each blow against the hard soil stripped more skin from her hands till they were slick with blood. Hour after hour she bent and twisted, feverish with the pain, until finally, aching, covered in mud and sweat, she planted the last potato in its hole. Darkness had long since fallen and she could barely see the ground she was standing on. But she had succeeded:

she had planted the last of the seedlings. On the brink of utter collapse they dragged themselves back to their shelter, weeping with exhaustion. For the time being the soldiers were content and left them unmolested, and the next morning Nayhouy watched her mother hobble over to rejoin the work gang on another field, whispering a silent word of thanks to the unknown God.

By 1979, Nayhouy's family were increasingly desperate to escape the brutal regime. She had watched hundreds of her neighbors and many of her own relatives succumb to starvation, beatings and overwork. Nayhouy's mother whispered her fears to Nayhouy one night. Though Nayhouy was just five years old, she would soon be recruited into the children's work gang to work all day long in the fields alongside the adults. Nayhouy wondered if she would be made to plant potatoes until her hands bled too, and quietly sobbed herself to sleep that night.

It was rumored that Vietnamese soldiers had defeated the Khmer Rouge further south and were getting closer every day, but the family had no stomach for more fighting and little hope that their ordeal would be over soon. They had heard furtive whispers of a truck driver who for an exorbitant price could get them near the Thai border. From there it would be a long trek through the jungle to a refugee camp. Whispered plans of escape began to fill their evenings.

One night a young cousin arrived exhausted from out of town. He came to Nayhouy's house in the shadows of the thatch shelter, "Your relatives sent me to get you and the rest of the family," he whispered breathlessly, "I can guide you to the refugee camp where they are. But we'll have to trek through the jungle...There are landmines..." he trailed off, staring at the floor. Nayhouy knew he wasn't certain they could make it.

Finally, a few days later, under the blazing midday sun, Nayhouy's mother gathered her into her arms, stroking Nayhouy's back and soothing her with whispers. Nayhouy's aunt carried her brother, now a toddler, and two or three other members of the family carried bags containing their meager possessions over their shoulders. Nayhouy watched her mother tuck some gold jewelry that she had carefully saved into the hem of her skirt and the tiny party hurried off to the appointed meeting place.

The truck was hours late, but finally they heard the low rumble of a distant vehicle rising from somewhere over the horizon. Eventually, a rusted heap piled high with fertilizer wheezed to a stop beside them and the nervous passengers climbed into the cab. The price in gold was negotiated and the truck set off.

Before long, the driver turned to Nayhouy's mother and poked a gnarled finger in her face, "You're my wife." His breath stunk. Turning to Nayhouy he flashed rotten yellow teeth, "And you're my daughter. You know...for when the Vietnamese soldiers stop us."

The truck growled and wheezed its way over the rutted mud roads. The Vietnamese army checkpoint was a nerve wracking game of bluff, before they were able to pass themselves off as a family accompanying their father and husband on a fertilizer delivery. Near the border with Thailand, the driver pulled his truck over and ushered them out onto the roadside verge that quickly blended into land-mine strewn jungle. With a jerk of his finger in the direction of Thailand, and a curt warning about the land-mines, the driver turned his truck around and was gone.

All that day, and through the night they trudged, stopping infrequently to rest and then pressing on before they were refreshed, fearful to stop too long. Every now and then the dark night would light up with a landmine explosion, either up ahead or behind them where they had already walked. Every step was a gamble with death. As they passed corpses, some recent victims, others just skeletons, bony fingers still clutching some treasured possession, Nayhouy's mother would cover Nayhouy's eyes with her fingers.

They waded through swollen streams and over steep mountain passes, always aware that a misstep might take them over a land-mine or Khmer Rouge booby trap. After days and nights, finally they stumbled into a makeshift military checkpoint. A wave of terror swept over them as a group of armed Cambodians trained their rifles on them. But it soon became apparent that these were not Khmer Rouge cadre, but one of the other militias that had sprung up along the Thai- Cambodian border. But these soldiers could also be just as unpredictable, just as rapacious, just as vicious.

"Please..." her mother began tearfully. But the soldiers were already gruffly waving them through. Another miracle. Nayhouy's mother gathered herself and motioned for the others in the party to hurry on.

They dared not speak for a few hundred meters, hurrying nervously out of rifle range. Then, the trees thinned and they saw it. A massive tent city. Blue tarpaulin as far as the eye could see. And everywhere, people. Thousands of people. Chatting and cooking over open fires, sitting around and laughing and just going about their daily business in a massive refugee camp, a seething mass of humanity. Nayhouy was confused, but her mother released a gasp, "We're safe!" And then in relief the two women, sisters-in-law, exhausted and filthy, collapsed into each others arms, crying and laughing, dancing round and round in gleeful abandon. Nayhouy at first just marveled at the laughter and then she joined in, delighted to see everyone so happy for the first time in so long. Nayhouy's mother gathered her into her arms and pressed her face to her daughter's cheek with a fierce affection, "Thank God. Thank God."

Following God Back Again

Nayhouy Greenfield

We never seemed to have enough to eat, even in the refugee camp. Somehow we survived those years of hunger, although the malnourishment my brother and I suffered left us shorter than average for our usually stocky family.

After a time in the refugee camp, we were selected to be relocated to the USA, but my uncle, who was living in New Zealand, was working with the refugee centre in Mangere, Auckland, and he arranged for us to join him there. My first memory of New Zealand is of eating a piece of cheese on the airplane (to this day I love cheese!).

I was teased constantly for my height (or lack or it), and being the shortest in the line I had to stand in the front of every single class photo. There were teachers who could never pronounce my name correctly. I felt out of place and like I never really could fit in.

But at the same time, God brought many people into our lives who loved us and shared Jesus with us by their prayers, words, and example. We had sponsors who adopted us as their 'grandchildren' and neighbors who took us to church with them and became our new aunties and uncles. They provided life-saving friendship and support for my mother, who—as a twenty-eight-year old widow with two young children, was in a strange land with a strange language, culture, people, and strange food. She worked long hours in a sewing factory while trying so hard to keep everything together for the three of us.

As the oldest, it was my job to be the interpreter: the one who went to the bank and paid the bills at age eight. I even went to my own parent-teacher interviews and interpreted my teacher's comments to my mother. I explained all the letters that came in, including my detention letters from school.

But through all these experiences, through all the culture shock and prejudice and kindnesses, I was always drawn back to Cambodia, the land of my birth, my people. As a Christian, this desire was to see God glorified in that country, to do something to contribute to God's healing and growing Kingdom there. From an early age, I started telling people that I was going to go back and be a missionary and a teacher. Meanwhile, God was developing in me a heart for young people, and especially for young people who had known hardship and suffering, just as I had.

After twenty years in New Zealand, including three years

teaching in South Auckland (the poorest and most ethnically diverse section of New Zealand's largest city), my husband, Craig, and I left the place that had become my 'home' to return to Cambodia and serve those who are called 'my people'.

In Cambodia, while living in a crowded tenement-building slum, Craig and I were led to start a ministry, now known as Project HALO (Hope, Assistance, Love for Orphans), in order to help children who had been orphaned by AIDS.[14] Servants was already working with adults suffering from AIDS, providing comfort and medicines to patients in the slums through the AIDS Home Care Program, but there was an urgent need to provide care for the kids who were being left behind as their parents died.[15] After a prolonged period of prayer and research into alternative models of care, we became convinced that building orphanages was not the best answer to this crisis, so we sought a more creative and long-term solution. Inspired in part by the sacrificial love I saw in my own mother, and in the many people God sent to help us in the refugee camp and while resettling in New Zealand, we decided on a more sustainable family and community-based model, one that would aim to keep children within extended families and their communities wherever possible.

Working with the existing AIDS Home Care ministry, we began to visit families in which the parents were dying, encouraging the children to discuss their feelings and their fears about their future. We gave each child a memory book, where they could place family photos and record memories before they were lost. With parents, uncles, aunts, grandparents and close neighbors - as well as with the children themselves - we discussed who the children wanted to live with in the future. At times, that meant recruiting Christian foster families or supporting teenager-headed households.

As we met together, focusing on who would love and nurture the children, the stigma of AIDS diminished. We helped parents write wills, guaranteeing the children's property rights. And after the death of the parents, we continued to follow-up with the children to make sure that the new family situation was working, that their rights were being respected, and that they were being fed, clothed and schooled properly. Volunteer 'youth mentors' were recruited from local churches to act as big brothers and big sisters to these children, taking them on social outings and working through their memory books to help them through the grief process.[16] With five full-time staff and numerous volunteers, Project HALO has so far provided friendship, mentoring and spiritual support to over 1,000 children.[17]

I like to think of the halo as a fitting symbol for my life. A symbol of God's protection and goodness over me. And like the halo, my life seems to have traveled full circle, bringing me back to the land I once fled - a land whose soil is stained with suffering, where the seeds of hope must now be sown amongst a new generation of children.

Om Kheun Forgives:
Concluding Reflections On Servanthood

Kristin Jack

Whoever among you wants to lead must become
the servant of all the others. (Mark 10:43)

Our first neighborhood in Cambodia was *Chrang Bak*, or "broken river-bank," a poor urban village perched right on the crumbling edge of the rubbish strewn Bassac River, one of the main branches of the Mekong river as it leaves Phnom Penh. With the annual monsoon rains from June through November, more of that river bank would turn to mud and collapse. As the river flooded, neighbors erected single plank footbridges to connect houses to higher ground. And when the flood waters rose higher still, the bridges would give way to small wooden boats that ferried us in and out of the community for a few cents. But the very poorest and most desperate would continue to wade through the turgid brown floodwaters year after year, in order to reach their ramshackle huts made from palm leaves, plywood, sheets of tin and cardboard that made up the village of *Chrang Bak*.[18]

Chrang Bak was close to the run-down local hospital where we worked in those early years, and we were charmed by its tall coconut palms and free-range pigs and chickens. Even though the river was chocolate brown - unlike the clear blue waters that flowed through our native New Zealand—it was still a river, and a small cooling breeze whispered off it, taking the edge from the sun's baking heat. A local family rented us a little shack for $20 a month, and after we paid them three years of advance rent, they built a new bamboo and palm leaf house next to ours, and then sunk a concrete-lined pit-latrine between our houses, which we shared.

We were the first Westerners to live in *Chrang Bak*, and the neighbors were fascinated and bemused by our presence among them. As with most poor communities, doors were always open and there was no concept of privacy, so we had a constant stream of visitors and new friends, which was great for our language learning and cultural immersion (though by the same token we had to work hard to cut out 'space' for ourselves).

In those early days, we felt completely safe and secure in our community. But then two of our neighbors were murdered, one on each side. The first neighbor was one of a handful of village alcoholics. Friendly enough when sober, he'd get emboldened every night by cheap rice-wine and start to complain and pick fights. One night, a man who was fed up with his ranting hit him over the head with a piece of scrap timber that had a rusty nail protuding. After a few days in a coma, our neighbor passed away. The man who'd killed him had to face a sentence in the grim Cambodian prison system, or else come up with $500 as compensation for the bereaved family. Our neighbor's widow, a gentle and long-suffering woman, had never seen so much money in all her life, and she actually seemed pretty happy with the deal.

On the other side of our house lived a lovely, dignified woman whom everyone called Ma Vibol, which means "mother of Vibol." Twenty-one-year-old Vibol, her eldest son, was bright and ambitious. As an apprentice goldsmith, his parents hoped that he would one day leave the slum and make a future for them all, blazing a trail for his younger sisters and providing for them in their old age. Ma Vibol's husband, whom she'd been forced to marry at gunpoint by Pol Pot's soldiers, was out of work and drank heavily.[19] Because Ma Vibol shared four children with her husband, and as he would simply follow her if she tried to leave him, she had decided to stay where she was and make the best of it. Vibol was her only hope.

One evening, as we were returning to our community past dark (the unwritten curfew, when most people retreated inside), we saw police armed with AK 47's clustered about 100 meters short of our house. As we approached, they glared at us, then allowed us to pass with a flick of the head. As we talked with the people milling around, we learned that two guys had jumped Vibol for his motorscooter, and when he had fought back, they had plunged knives into his back and throat. Though the struggle had taken place in front of a line of busy shanty shops and dirt-floored coffee bars, nobody had intervened, no doubt wanting to avoid getting dragged in.[20]

Someone did rush to Ma Vibol's home, but by the time she and her husband arrived, the attackers had fled on the motorscooter, and their son lay dying in a pool of blood. They gathered him up in their arms, and as Vibol's dad drove to the hospital, Ma Vibol clung on behind, cradling her son in her arms, begging him to stay alive. As they pulled their motor scooter to a stop outside the hospital, Ma Vibol knew that it was too late. Having lost so much blood, he had died in her arms.

Two days later we attended Vibol's funeral, along with most everyone in the village. Vibol's body lay in a coffin covered with flowers, photos and candles in the small, sparsely furnished wooden stilt house where he had lived with his family. In the corner, a TV played clips from a video of Vibol, a few weeks before, leading his younger sisters and other children in a traditional Khmer dance at the village New Year celebration.[21]

Several men strained to lower the coffin down the ladder-like steps from the house, and then we all fell into line behind the coffin. Carrying flowers, we trouped with the monks to the local temple, where Vibol was cremated in a simple Buddhist ceremony. Vibol's mother, shrouded in white, worked hard to maintain her usual dignity and composure, but periodically her face would crumple and convulse with tears.

Vibol's father, strangely dispassionate, filmed the ceremony with a video camera (a gift, like the TV and VCR, from relatives in the United States). Smiling often, he thanked his neighbors for coming with slurred speech. From that day on, he drank himself into a state of permanent intoxication that even sleep could not relieve.

The police never caught Vibol's assailants, though witness accounts clearly identified them, so they "arrested" the father of the main suspect, refusing to let him go until Vibol's family had been paid $800 in compensation, along with a replacement motorscooter. Again, the accused family somehow scraped it together, but Vibol's parents gained no relief from this compensation. Gradually, Ma Vibol's name reverted to *Om* ("aunty") *Kheun* (her first name), a title of affection and respect.

After Vibol's death, in the midst of her own pain and poverty, Om Kheun carried herself with compassion and wisdom. As a local shop keeper (a simple wooden shack with rough shelves from which she sold small quantities of vegetables and other essentials like cooking oil, sugar and dried fish), many people came to her for foodstuffs as well as advice. When very poor neighbors - whose children she could hear crying from hunger at night - came to buy food on credit, she could not say no.

With our small Christian cell group that met in the village, we often prayed for Om Kheun and often invited her to join us. Though she asked about what we were studying, she would smile and tell us about the comfort she found in the Buddhism that had held her family together for generations. She was especially proud of a nephew who was a practicing monk in the United States, serving the Khmer refugee community there. 'All moral paths lead to God in the end', she would remind us.

One day, seven years after we first moved into *Chrang Bak*, Om Kheun came to visit us. Her voice trembling with emotion, she told us that from her grocery shop, she had been watching everybody in the village - in particular those who called themselves followers of Jesus. After seven years of watching, she had decided that she wanted to serve this Jesus. The local monks, she told us, had never visited again after her son's funeral. And later, at personal expense, she had helped cook food at a big temple festival. Again, no monks had come to visit her or thank her. But nearly every week, one or two of the local Christians asked how she was and invited her to join them.

A few weeks later, after eagerly attending our cell group gatherings, Om Kheun dropped in and shared that she had learned from the gospels that Jesus calls us to forgive those who have wronged us. With this new insight, she had examined her heart and found that there was something tainting her relationships in the village. Over the years she had extended so much credit to other families that it now amounted to hundreds of dollars (a huge amount in a little slum economy). Om Kheun realized that she felt angry and frustrated with those who owed her so much, because she would be so much further ahead in life if they paid their debts. But she also realized that those poor families were deeply ashamed of the debts they would never be able to repay, and they avoided her as much as possible. She neither wanted to feel bitter, nor be avoided. Inspired by what she read in the gospels, she decided to wipe the slate clean. Taking her record book in hand, she went from family to family, and before their eyes drew a line through their debt, declaring it 'forgiven'. At the stroke of a pen, they were set free – and so was she.

Om Kheun's life could have ended up marked by bitterness and hatred. She continues to struggle with her husband's alcoholism and with raising three daughters in a place of abject poverty and violence. Some days are still filled with tears, but Om Kheun senses that God is using her to bring healing to others. She was recently recruited to be kitchen manager in a restaurant set-up by a Christian entrepreneur. She also works with an indigenous Khmer organization that trains young women in life skills. Recently, she began appearing weekly on national television, demonstrating the preparation of beautiful Cambodian dishes. These roles are enabling Om Kheun to fulfill two of her greatest passions in life: cooking delicious food and nuturing the teenage staff placed under her, all of whom have come from urban poor neighborhoods, and many of whom became orphans after AIDS snatched away their parents. By mothering these teenagers and living out a life of love and beauty, Om Kheun has found something far better than the bitterness that could so easily have destroyed her. She found a God who is neither aloof nor impassive in the face of our suffering, but one who enters fully into it, offering hope and forgiveness in place of despair.

In every community we enter, there are pearls of great beauty waiting to be uncovered. Unofficial leaders and community organizers, networkers and elders. People who love their neighbors and who serve the poor. Worthy men and women of peace. Jesus instructed his disciples to look for these special folk as one of the first steps in their mission (Matthew 10:11; Luke 10:6). Paul was an expert at finding these people: Timothy, Lydia, Jason, Aquila, Priscilla and so on. Each place we go, God has already been at work, and it is our task and privilege to join in with what He is doing. We need to ask God to show us who these special people are, and then invite them to join us as co-workers in God's Kingdom. This lengthy, prayerful process requires patience, but what could be more satisfying than helping others realize that they are God's sons and daughters, beautiful people created in His image for a future of hope and purpose, freedom and dignity? Most of the other things we devote our lives to seem very trivial by comparison to this great task: to be His ambassadors, imploring others to be reconciled with Him, with one another, and with themselves.

Acts of Beauty, Acts of Humanity
Mark 14:1-11

There were glimmers of beauty
in your tears of shame
that fell like silver
that fell like rain
a jar is broken
pouring out its all
into this story, history
our story, her story,
preparing for death
pleading for life
with a fragrance that makes
hard places grow soft,
by calling for mercy
from those keeping the score
from those counting the cost
from those knowing the law.
But a heart stripped naked
is revealing real truth
that runs deeper and cleaner
than shame or profanity,
it's revealing a beauty,
the divine-broken image
in one woman's humanity.

SERVANTHOOD

1. Matthew 20:28.
2. Mark 10:43.
3. See John 15:15.
4. Mark 9:23 and 29.
5. Romans 12:14-21.
6. Shabu is an amphetamine, similar to "crack," which is synthetically produced, cheap and readily available. It's known as the "poor man's cocaine."
7. Onesimo is the drug rehabilitation ministry for teenagers described in "Ricco – a boy in search of his father," by Christian Schneider, found in section 2 (Community).
8. In many parts of Asia, toothpaste is looked upon as a medicine and is used as a cheap first-aid treatment for skin lesions and burns. This is a dangerous practice that easily leads to infections and secondary damage.
9. 64,936 people per square kilometer (www://unicef.org/infocountry 2004).
10. Filthy and dangerous as it was, few wanted to leave their homes and livelihoods on Smokey Mountain. Nevertheless, the residents of Smokey Mountain were forcibly—and violently, in some instances—relocated to "temporary housing," where they are waiting for the Government to move them into new apartments that were promised as compensation. Some of these families have been waiting for more than ten years. When the families finally move, the rent on the new homes will most likely exceed their incomes. The land that was reclaimed by the Government has been developed commercially, and the big companies that moved in generate huge incomes for their owners and managers, all of whom live many kilometers away in green and spacious suburbs.
11. Sniffing glue is common among slum kids. The glue acts as a hunger suppressant as well as an anesthetic. A can of glue, which can be bought for a few pesos and then divided up amongst a group of friends, is cheaper than food.
12. Since most former drug users were HIV positive and anti-retroviral drugs were not widely available at this time, the Servants team could not prevent these young Thais from dying, but they did ensure that they died knowing they were loved. When acute symptoms flared up that required specific medical attention, those who lived at the House of Life for the duration of their illness would be taken to one of Bangkok's public hospitals, accompanied by someone from the team to provide nursing and pastoral care.
13. Most of the people who contract AIDS are abandoned—even by their families—because the shame of AIDS is too great.
14. By the mid 1990s, Cambodia had the fastest spread of the HIV virus in all of Asia, though thankfully this figure has been lowered since.
15. There are an estimated 80,000 children (amongst 470,000 orphans) in Cambodia whose parents have died from AIDS (www://unicef.org/infocountry 2005).
16. The Evangelical Fellowship of Cambodia, an umbrella group for the majority of Cambodia's new churches, has adopted the 'big brothers/big sisters' component of HALO as a part of their official strategy and are encouraging churches throughout Cambodia to replicate this kind of ministry as a response to the AIDS epidemic.
17. Read the full story behind Project HALO, Craig and Nayhouy's adventures in Cambodia, and their research into community versus orphanage based care of children in Craig's book Urban Halo, published by Authentic Media (2007), or visit www.urbanhalo.org
18. After three years of living there, the land that our own little house stood on was completely washed away!
19. In the late 1970s, the Khmer Rouge realised they needed to repopulate the country after killing so many of their own people, and so they began arbitrarily pairing couples off, declaring them married, and demanding that they produce children for Onkaa (the "Organisation"), the faceless nom de plume for Pol Pot.
20. Fear rules in Cambodia and is one of Pol Pots many crippling legacies.
21. Traditional Khmer dancing is graceful and slow, full of subtle gestures and fluid hand movements.

Five

SIMPLICITY

Nothing is more clear than that Jesus Christ walked in well-nigh amazing simplicity of life. He was centered in God and had a transparency towards God that ordered everything. Simplicity is part of what it means to be a follower of Christ. To be sure, the cost of simplicity is great, but the cost of duplicity is greater. Duplicity costs the joyful communion with divine Center, faith that sees everything in the light of God's governance for good, abiding peace, and the ability to walk cheerfully over the face of the earth in the power of the Lord. In short, it costs the abundant life that Jesus said he came to bring. Simplicity may be difficult, but the alternative is immensely more difficult.

Richard Foster[1]

INTRODUCTION: FINDING FREEDOM

Kristin Jack

So do not worry, saying, 'What shall we eat?' or 'What shall we drink?' or 'What shall we wear?' For the pagans run after all these things, and your heavenly Father knows that you need them. But seek first his kingdom and his righteousness, and all these things will be given to you as well. (Matthew 5:31-33)

Our own planet is telling us that we are living beyond our means: our ever increasing consumption has precipitated an escalating environmental crisis. Even our economies are telling us we are living beyond our means. The recent global financial crisis has reminded us that greed is never a smart foundation upon which to build our lives or our communities.

Mother Teresa, picking up on Gandhi's words, often reminded us that "we must live simply in order that others may simply live." And that we might allow our ecosystems to survive and flourish for future generations. Jesus tells us that a commitment to pursuing spiritual wealth ahead of material accumulation is actually the key to finding true freedom in this life. It makes sense. By living simply we release resources that can be used to help those for whom even three good meals a day remains a dream. By being churches, missions and organizations that keep overheads low, refusing to spend more money on ourselves than is absolutely necessary, we free up resources that become life-giving for our most desperate neighbors.

And, of course, we all agree. We read Christ's words – laden with warnings for the rich and promises for the poor – and nod our heads in mental assent. And yet, as soon as we have put down our Bibles, so often we go straight back to doing the opposite: climbing career ladders, chasing success and status, and accumulating far more 'stuff' than we'll ever actually need. As churches we are sure we need the latest, greatest sound-system or LCD projector in order to be relevant.

How can this be? Why are we so blind to our own wealth and other people's desperate need? Where does this hideous blindness - that could one day drag us to hell if Jesus' words are accurate (e.g. Matthew 25:31-46) - where does it come from?

One of the main problems is that we simply do not see our selves as rich. Surely it's not us who Jesus is talking about in these passages? Surely he is having a go at the 'super-rich', the top 5% of society, or the top 10%, or even the top 20%, but certainly not us!

And indeed, in comparison with those above us, we may not seem rich. We're forever looking at others, seeing what they have: the type of car, size or location of their house, clothes, cell phone and so on, and saying to ourselves, *"There are lots of people in the world who have much more than I do."* There is something in human nature that tempts us to look with envy at those who are better off than ourselves, rather than to look out with empathy at those who have so much less.

But the reality for most of us who are educated enough to read this book, let alone buy it, is that we are very, very rich. This reality is always obscured when we waste time comparing ourselves with the super-wealthy within Western society, a sickening comparison of envy that the advertisers encourage us to make. But as soon as we compare ourselves to the wider world Jesus calls us to love, embrace and minister to, it becomes starkly apparent that we are, in fact, very rich. According to the World Bank Development Research Group, if our yearly income is US $25,400 per annum, then we're in the top 10% of the world's wealthiest. If we earn US $33,700 per annum, then we're in the top 5% of worlds wealthiest.[2] Who among us can honestly deny that we are, in fact, those *"who are well fed now"* (Luke 6:25)?

Nominally, Christians make up about one-third of the world's population, but earn about two-thirds of the world's income. They spend about 97 percent of that on themselves, only giving away the remaining 3 percent of their income.[3] According to Jesus, this sort of giving isn't terribly meritorious - he seeks from us a generosity of giving that far exceeds that. Charles Wesley, evangelist and founder of the Methodists, understood the radicalism of Christ's teaching on wealth when he said, "If I die with more than 10 pounds still in my pocket, call me a liar and a thief, for I have betrayed the gospel."

However, the goal of Jesus' teaching on wealth, giving and simplicity isn't to condemn us or make us feel helpless. Quite the opposite: Jesus gave his teaching in order to lead us from bondage into freedom, so that we could find truly abundant life. So change is possible, but it will take considerable help from others and from God, for mammon is a dark spiritual force with considerable powers of addiction.[4]

The freedom Jesus offers us consists of both inner and outer simplicity. These are not burdens, but precious gifts he offers us. It is our hope that the stories in this section will inspire and encourage you in your journey along the path towards freedom from the idolatry of greed[5] and the deceitfulness of wealth.[6] At the end of Reuben and Kim's story, "The Gift of Simple Living: Learning from Our Children," there are six simple steps you can take to lead you on the road toward freedom and the abundant life that Jesus' promised to all who would pick up their cross and follow him.

The Gift of Friendship:
Learning from our Neighbors

Sal

(India)

Sal, an Occupational Therapist from New Zealand, lived for several years with her husband, Gregg, a rock climber, outdoor educationalist and physics teacher, and their three children in both Delhi and Kolkata. After returning to New Zealand, they have since moved to Bolivia and are again working amongst the poor there.

I met Sunita as soon as we moved into the slum. She was an outgoing, friendly girl of sixteen with an eight-month-old baby.

She hated to be alone, and so while she was cooking in her little hut, she would come and ask me to join her. I would amuse her little girl as she cooked, while also providing entertainment for the other neighborhood kids who would poke their heads in to stare at this bideshi (foreigner). My Bengali was limited, but because Sunita was so good at speaking simply and slowly, we covered a wide range of topics, laughed together, and shared our joys and sorrows. Sunita offered me the gift of her friendship when I desperately needed a friend in that harsh place.

Sunita lived with her parents, siblings, husband and child in a house made of dung and mud (most of the other houses in our area were brick) with a tarpaulin for a roof. It was stifling hot in summer, freezing cold in winter, and wet during the monsoons. Sunita and her husband sometimes tried to move out to their own little room, but inevitably they'd fall behind with the rent and have to shift back in with her family.

In winter, when the temperature sometimes dropped to zero degrees celsius, we would give out blankets to street people, who might otherwise die from the cold. Sunita found out about our little project and asked if she could have a blanket too, as her daughter was cold at night. I would often find her huddling over a smoky fire. Her family couldn't afford wood or even dung to burn, but during the summer they would collect any garbage and put it on top of their roof, drying it to be burnt in the winter, when it produced acrid smoke and an awful stench.

Soon after we met she told me that hers was a 'love marriage' rather than an arranged one. Her parents were actually quite happy because that had lifted a degree of the financial burden off them, since they hadn't had to pay a dowry. However, it had also left the family feeling scorned by the wider community, which was exacerbated by the fact that they were the poorest people in our neighborhood. Another advantage of this 'love marriage' was that Sunita and her husband lived with her parents instead of his (the traditional arrangement), thus offering her protection from the abuse and beatings so common in other marriages.

Sunita seemed to go against the current with many of the

conventions. In poor Bengali society, women always wear Saris after they marry, no matter how young they are. But Sunita insisted on wearing the Punjabi suits worn by the unmarried. Other women I befriended had so little freedom. They went from being controlled by their fathers to being controlled by their husbands.

When the supplier was about to turn off the power in the tiny room they were living in, Sunita became furious with her husband, because he wouldn't give her the ten rupees that were needed. I begged her to take those ten rupees from me, but she refused. "No," she stormed, "it's my husband's responsibility."

One day I invited three friends to visit a market as my guests. The entrance fee of 5 rupees (25 cents) was designed to keep poor people out, and of the three, only Sunita was brave enough to come. I wondered how she'd cope with an eight-month-old, out and about and wearing no nappies, but she simply brought along several changes of clothes for him. It was a joy to see Sunita delight in all the beautiful craft stalls and simple but delicious eating places. She had been born in this slum but had never been further than the local school or the *boroloks* (rich man's) house, where she worked as a servant.

Despite our commitment to incarnation, I have to admit that Gregg and I eventually grew tired of curries for breakfast, lunch and dinner. So before long, I began cooking mashed potatoes with cauliflower and cheese or pasta for dinner. Most of our visitors would taste the foreign food and then quickly decline our invitation for a meal, but not Sunita. She was undoubtedly more adventurous than most of our neighbors, but her main motivation was simple hunger. She had a beautiful, healthy breast-fed baby, but she herself was skin and bones. Most days she would eat only a small amount of rice or *roti* (unleavened bread).

On my birthday Sunita arrived with a bunch of flowers, a gift of love that filled my eyes with tears. I knew that she earned a mere five rupees an hour, that her work was periodic, and that she never saw any money from her husband.

Just as we were preparing to go on home leave, after which we would then move on to another Indian city, word came that our slum had been listed for demolition. For a family like Sunita's, who didn't own their hut, there would be no recompense, nothing to help them build a new life elsewhere. When I returned to visit five months later, their home had been bulldozed, and they were in another tiny room waiting for that to be bulldozed too. Sunita was working really long hours while her mum looked after the baby. I arrived to visit with our new three-month-old baby, and Sunita immediately told me to wait and rushed off. Twenty minutes later she arrived back with a gift for Toby, then bustled around, cooking us all an evening meal.

As I left I handed her an envelope and said it was a letter to read later. I was hardly ten steps away when she ran after me, saying I wasn't to give her money, insisting that I take it back. It was so little, but I just wanted to give something to help them out. I told her she was my very good friend, that I didn't know when I'd see her again, and I just wanted to give her a little gift. She finally accepted it with tears in her eyes.

I never saw her again. The next time I returned to visit there was no slum and no Sunita. There was no one to tell me where she had gone. Our friendship taught me about living in a slum with a child and how to cope without all the paraphernalia we think so necessary in the West. She taught me about generosity, about giving that is truly sacrificial. She taught me not to take life too seriously, but to find joy even when worries are piling up around you.

I pray that the Jesus we so often talked about will reveal Himself to her more and more, and that she will be able to turn to him whenever life grows too hard.

The Gift of Time: Learning from the Poor

Wendy Hing-Mather

(Manila, Philippines)

Wendy, her husband, Paul, and their four children lived among Manila's urban poor for over ten years, beginning in the early 1990s. They continue to be deeply involved with community building in Porirua (Wellington), New Zealand. Wendy, a gifted teacher, mentor and counselor, works with women escaping domestic violence, and Paul works with Praxis, an urban mission training program.

In the early morning hours of Christmas in 1997, Vivienne, the young woman who lived next to us, gave birth to a baby boy in her small plywood home. Her three children, ages three-and-a-half, two and one, lay contentedly asleep, oblivious to the arrival of their new brother. Lito, Vivienne's husband, had gone out earlier in search of a midwife, too ashamed to call on the one living in their community because they had taken so long to pay her fees for the previous child's birth. When he had finally paid for that birth, it had been with borrowed money. After several hours, the husband was still gone, and as Vivienne gazed at her newly born baby, something didn't seem to be quite right. The placenta had come out with the baby and was covering his face as he struggled to take his first breath. Then the baby went quiet, Vivienne told us later as she wept. Without the support of her husband or midwife, Vivienne hadn't known how to help her baby, and his precious life was unnecessarily lost.

There is no professional counseling service available for Vivienne, so we - and many others in the community - tried to listen to her and stand with her family as they grieved.

Like so many others who live in poverty, Vivienne and Lito have learned about the fragility of life. Their lack of resources has taught them to rejoice in each day of life as a fleeting gift - and also about how to live in surrendered acceptance whenever death snatches a loved one away.

One afternoon, I dropped by Reby's make-shift house in front of the local church. Three pieces of roofing iron were supported by a pre-existing concrete wall on one side and some old bits of timber on the other. Her belongings were crammed into a few cardboard boxes and plastic bags stored beneath this structure. As we chatted about the pain and powerlessness she felt in being evicted from her previous squatter home, feelings of inadequacy and impotency overwhelmed me. I couldn't think of any comforting words or wise advice. I had so little to offer, except my time and listening ear.

As she lay before me the bare, hard facts of her life, her face broke into a broad smile and she spoke of her hope that soon she might be able to move into a half-built shack in a nearby squatter area. I sat next to her in silence, struggling with questions about what I could do to help, with all my access to resources.

Then, pulling out a bag, Reby proudly showed me the embroidery she was working on. In between washing clothes by hand, sending her children off to school, and facing the ongoing uncertainties about where her next home would be and where her family's next meal would come from, she had made time to make something beautiful. There was so much I needed to learn from her. With amazing courage and resilience, Reby's will to survive kept her living - with hope and beauty - in this narrow place where I doubted I would have been able to. But the difference between Reby and me was that she had no other option.

SIMPLICITY

The Gift of Suffering:
Learning from Our Own Journeys

Efren and Becky Roxas

(Manila, Philippines; Phnom Penh, Cambodia)

Efren and Becky Roxas are pastors, teachers, missionaries, and mentors. After ministering among the urban poor of Manila for twenty-one years, they moved to Cambodia in 2006 to serve the poor in Phnom Penh by ministering to families, couples with marital difficulties, the young men in TASK's Teenage Drug Users Rehabilitation ministry and TASK staff. Like others who have known poverty and suffering first-hand, Efren and Becky are able to preach the "good news" with empathy, compassion and a willingness to rough it for the sake of the gospel.

Like many Filipinos, Efren grew up in a rural province, as one of eight children of poor tenant rice farmers, subsisting on a fifth of all they grew, while the other fourfifths went to enriching their landlord. Even as a small child, Efren's labor was essential to the family, and some of his earliest memories are of tending water buffalo, sitting astride them as they grazed under the fierce sun. But Efren yearned to learn, and as he labored in the mud of the rice paddies, he daydreamed of the freedom that education might bring to him.

After completing primary school, however, Efren's parents told him they could not afford the books and fees for school, nor could they do without his help on the farm. Efren did his duty, working long hard hours every day, but inside he grieved the loss of his chance for a brighter future. He vowed that if he ever got the chance to study again, he would let nothing deter him. A year later, his family's fortunes improved, and his parents allowed him to return to school. Efren worked hard and did well, eventually gaining a scholarship to study chemical engineering at one of Manila's top colleges.

179

Like millions of other rural Filipino's, Efren bundled up his meager belongings and set off for a new life in Manila with high hopes. Fear and excitement jostled inside him as the decrepit bus left the rice paddies behind and eventually lurched into the fume-filled highways and concrete canyons of the sprawling capital city.

Though tuition was free, Efren had to work part-time to pay for food, clothing and rent. He rose at 4:00 am, prepared breakfast and enough food for his other two meals, then set off at 5:00, battling on buses through Manila's choking traffic, to reach his college by 7:00. Classes ended midday, after which Efren raced off to his hospital janitor's job, which didn't finish until 10:00 pm. Efren threw himself into his studies whole-heartedly, snatching study time in the evening as he cleaned. Sympathetic nurses helped find him quiet rooms to study in, calling him out if there was a 'cleaning emergency' somewhere, such as a patient's death, since it was part of Efren's job to wash down the deceased's body.

But this disciplined, grueling routine wore Efren down physically and emotionally. Desperate to keep up with his studies and feeling terribly alone, he joined a fraternity in his third year, hoping the older students would give him advice, guidance and social support. The senior student leader of the fraternity took a special interest in Efren, but he was heavily into the drug scene and invited Efren to share drugs with him. As Efren consumed increasing quantities of alcohol, cannabis, valium and amphetamines, his grades deteriorated, and he became so unreliable in his work at the hospital that he was fired. As his life collapsed into darkness, Efren met Becky, a young accounting (and later teaching) student, who also came from a poor rural family, and she became the one point of stability during this tumultuous period.

After falling deeply in love, Becky and Efren were married, and their first child followed quickly. Though Efren repeatedly vowed that he would stop drinking and using drugs, his habit was stronger than his will-power. Crises, arguments and fights plagued their marriage as the little money that he and Becky made as part-time security guards was squandered by his addictions.

One day Becky came home from work to find Efren slumped

drunkenly in front of the TV. Enraged at yet another broken promise, Becky stormed upstairs and grabbed Efren's shotgun out of the bedroom. Flying back down the stairs screaming, she advanced on Efren with the gun pointed straight at him. A sudden wave of sobriety swept over Efren, and he leapt out of the nearest window and into the street, running for his life. (He didn't know that Becky had unloaded the gun upstairs.)

They still loved each other deeply, and so after a few weeks, they moved back together again, but their relationship was in pieces. Desperate to save his marriage, Efren embarked on a search for some source of help greater than himself, and he began attending a seeker's study at the Bahai church near his house.[7] He loved these discussion times, and was particularly captivated by the teachings of the prophet Jesus, in part because of his own family's Catholic background. Over and over, he would ask the discussion leader to expand on Jesus' teachings, or to explain more about what they meant. Exasperated, the Bahai leader told Efren to get hold of a Bible and start studying it. Shortly after this conversation, Efren discovered that another of his neighbors was a very devout Catholic. Studying the Bible with this neighbor, Efren began to understand the Christian message more clearly, but he was still unable to shake his addictions.

Then one Saturday morning, as Efren was flipping through TV channels, he came across a preacher telling the story of the prodigal son (Luke 15:11-31), and the words gripped him. *He* was that son who had wandered away and become lost. *He* was the one who had forsaken the promises of his youth, and now was wallowing in the refuse of a wasted life. As tears rolled down Efren's cheeks, the TV preacher invited his studio audience to raise their hands if they knew it was time for them to come back to God. Crying out to God for forgiveness, Efren raised his hand, then fell on his knees and gave himself to God, his Father.

After a five-year addiction, Efren knew that God would give him the power to beat his drug problem. He and Becky went to stay with Becky's parents in the countryside for several weeks. There, Efren rose early and walked to the nearby beach to renew his commitment to God and to living drug-free. He began to discipline his body with exercise and farm work and to discipline his mind with prayer and meditation on the Scriptures.

On his return to Manila with Becky, Efren joined the charismatic Christian church in his neighborhood, which taught that as God's children, we can expect to live lives of increasing health, material prosperity and continuous blessing.[8] At first, this emphasis on having "victory" in Christ helped Efren gain a sense of confidence that he and God were bigger and stronger than his addictions, which were under control now. But even though he was praying and studying the Scriptures daily, attending church, tithing faithfully, working harder than ever and doing everything that the pastor said one should do in order to grow prosperous, he and Becky were still desperately poor. As he looked around the church, Efren noticed that the 'health, wealth and prosperity' doctrine that the pastor continuously preached only seemed to be working for the leaders of the church and the handful of middle-class members. The poor always remained poor.

As Efren attended church and Bible studies, he said very little to Becky about his conversion, having decided that she should be able to see that the changes in his life were genuine before she heard it from his lips. He had broken too many promises and let her down too many times for his words to convince her. For her part, Becky spent these months watching Efren carefully, looking to see if this was for real or not. After a year, Becky made up her mind to follow Jesus.

For two years, Efren and Becky continued to be involved in this 'prosperity gospel' church, but then a Servants missionary moved into their community. Efren and Becky were amazed to see how these 'rich Christians' from the West were prepared to give up their lives of privilege to live amongst the poor, fully immersing themselves in the life of their neighborhood. Their first assessment of these Servants workers was that they were crazy and eccentric. But then one day, their oldest daughter became very sick, and Hugh Todd came to visit their little home in the slum.[9] He spent time praying for them, assisted their family through a desperate financial situation and also helped when Efren came down with acute appendicitis. Hugh visited often, discussing with Efren the turbulent Filipino political situation and what the Bible had to say about it all.[10] As Hugh became a dear friend,[11] Becky and Efren witnessed his genuine servanthood and deep love for Christ, and they were challenged to consider how they might start loving the poorest people in their community.

As they wrestled with these questions, they began to discover that even though they were regarded as "poor and weak," they had gifts to offer their neighbors because of God's work in their lives. Just as God had empowered Efren, he could now empower others. When Efren and Becky began to look for a church that would truly serve and empower the poor, the Servants missionaries asked Efren to consider leading one of the churches they had planted in that community.

After much prayer and discussion, Efren began pastoring a Living Springs Church,[12] ministering to the desperately needy people in his community spiritually, emotionally, physically and economically - not just on Sundays, but every day of the week. Eager for more teaching and equipping, he looked into the established Bible schools and seminaries, but felt that they couldn't help pastors like him, because their entry requirements were too high and too expensive. Moreover, the curriculum was too academic and theoretical, addressing abstract theological issues rather than the day-to-day life crises that abounded in these communities. What's more, these Bible schools asked for full-time attendance, but he was needed by his community for active ministry during the week. Eventually, Efren came to the Servants team and asked if they could begin an informal, part-time theological training program for urban poor church and community leaders, one that addressed the real issues that he and other Living Springs church pastors faced each day. From this seed, Lilok[13] was born, a place where people could come two or three days a week to learn from each other and from more experienced facilitators.

For the next twenty-one years, God used Efren and Becky to raise up and empower leaders, who in turn empowered others. Efren also served at-risk and drug-addicted youth through Onesimo,[14] where his own tumultuous life journey was deeply relevant.

Then, in the late-1990s, Efren heard about the un-reached peoples further afield in Asia, and he felt strongly challenged to start praying for Buddhist communities. In that same year, he and Becky hosted a Khmer visitor from Servants Cambodia, who they orientated to the Living Springs work among the urban poor. Remembering how deeply they had been impacted by the cross-cultural, incarnational ministry of the Servants missionaries who moved into their community, they began to sense God leading them towards cross-cultural mission, and eventually felt God calling them to Cambodia.

In July of 2006 they were commissioned and sent out to an urban poor community in Phnom Penh by their church and Filipino co-workers.[15] Moving from one urban poor background to another has made the cross-cultural transition for Efren and Becky easier than it is for many Western missionaries, since they were already accustomed to the heat, dirt, noise, over-crowding, lack of privacy, suffering, and overwhelming needs of their neighbors. They had already had much practice at living creatively in the tension between battling injustice and relying on grace. Moreover, at first glance, many assume they are Cambodians, and so there's less expectation that they have come with big financial resources. Of course, pulling up deep roots from the Philippines has been wrenching for them, and they now face two cross-cultural challenges: building new relationships with the Khmer people as well as with their Western Servants teammates. Even though their friendship and church networks in the Philippines have been amazingly generous, raising financial support has been a struggle (more than it would be for someone from the wealthy West), since many of their supporters come from urban poor communities. And yet Efren and Becky know that where God calls, he equips and provides, and they trust Him to keep leading them, confident that the beautiful work He has begun in them...will carry on till the day of completion (Philippians 1:3-6).

The Gift of Home: Learning from the Location

Miriam Hadcocks

(United Kingdom)

After spending a month as an intern with the Servants team in Cambodia in 2004, Miriam returned to England determined to live out the Servants principles in her own community. She is now an integral part of the Servants team in the UK, and when she is not spending time with anarchists and street kids, she is busy trying to recruit folk to the Servants cause.

"Not got your usual lift today then?" said Reg, the undeservedly maligned Asian shop keeper.

"No not today," she said from under her blue-rinse. And taking her change, she set off slowly into the car park.

Hurriedly I bought my things and rushed after her. This was exactly why I had intentionally moved to this south Abingdon neighborhood, hoping to build links with the community, yet everything English about me said to ignore her. Eventually, trying to look as little like a hand-bag stealer as possible, I approached. "Excuse me, would you like a lift home with that?"

Sitting in my purple caravan on the driveway in Saxton Road, amongst the most notorious houses in town, I think about how deeply I have come to know and love this place. South Abingdon, with all its madness and mad characters, may look pretty, sitting on the Thames like the vast number of serene swans that live here, but under the surface, it's kicking frantically to stay afloat. I remember the moments when I've been scared: sleeping in this ill-protected caravan after a break in; listening to the sound of shouting at night; the brick through my window that missed my face by inches; waiting for the local gang to burn the caravan with me in it after I'd received their threat, but chose to stay and talk it through with them (they never came). I think of all the pain I've witnessed: the girl badly beaten only ten yards away, the fights between two drug addict friends that left both permanently scarred,

185

the drug overdoses, suicides, infant deaths and miscarriages. And the pain I've experienced myself. The vulnerability of being threatened six times with eviction. The frustration of working when nothing seems to happen and everything is unquantifiable. The disappointment of false starts. The isolation of trying to get people to join a project they can't understand. The waning motivation to prayerwalk alone - yet again. The painful separation I've felt from many who share the same faith, but not the same vision. I have been lower this year than in ages, but isn't that the point of incarnation, community and wholism—that what effects one effects all?

But in spite of all the pain, the abiding images I carry are of joy, relationship, transformation. I think of the moment two neighbors spoke to me for the first time, after I'd been living here for nine months. Or the time my addict friend shrugged off ridicule in order to help me fix my recently-broken window. I remember sitting with the local Nazi (his word for himself, not mine) as he wept for the mother he lost fourteen years ago. Playing poker for matches with a ten-year-old whose mother had kicked him out again. Watching the lad with a reputation for burning boats and trashing cars pick up litter and then offer to clean my car for free (he didn't nick it). My conversation with two young lads who were hiding from the police. The various art projects I've done with the local kids. How I left a job I loved and turned down a brilliant, well-paid job because they weren't local enough and took up too much time - only to be offered an eighteen-hour job at the local family centre. The bring-your-own-tree party (a story in itself). The conversation I had as I built the Servants slum house in the front garden, and the eleven-year-old who then decided to give all her clothes and old toys to Oxfam (if her mum sees this, I'll deny everything...). Being called on in emergencies because, "You're always the one who helps." How much more it has helped me to know that people can come to me.

And then there has been the plain ridiculous. Saying, "she's likely to put a crow bar through the window," as a crow bar came flying through the window. Moral dilemmas as to whether I should encourage my friend to modify her behavior as I helped her sew the seven-foot high wings for her nude vampire modeling shoot. Chatting with a police officer like a good citizen, surrounded by stolen rosebushes (they were going to be bull-dozed). Prayer walking bare foot 'cause it worked for St Francis (shame I picked November). Giving an old caravan to a homeless guy who then demolished it to make a trailer for his motorbike and decided he didn't want it. Chasing a Jack Russell terrier by car. Pony riding down Sakky (slang for Saxton Road, the name of the local gang and an insult hurled at the locals).

But mainly, what remains is God: He was here first, and pops up in unlikely places. Like the selfless actions of a skin-headed, voodoo practicing friend. Or the faith, love, support, prayer and evangelism of a follower of Christ who is adamant that there is no God. Or a stoned Scottish giant who has a seven-year mission to bring about the apocalypse but still finds time to love people and the world around him. These are my "men and women of peace." In them, I see God and hear His voice.

As my first year of watching and waiting ends, Sakky has become "SACCCI", the name of the South Abingdon Community Co-operative Credit Initiative, the goods, skills and community activity exchange that my friends and I are starting, along with SANE (South Abingdon News Exchange), a local newsletter. The council says people are now choosing to live here. Attitudes have changed as locals talk about community and start co-operatively buying organic goods.

As I enter my second year, I'm facing another eviction, and there is still a long way to go with SACCCI and SANE. And I wonder if any of this really 'works' anyway. But sitting in my purple, aluminum bubble of love, I'm glad I chose to give that old lady a lift home, and I'm glad God placed me here.

The Gift of Beauty: Celebrating God's Creation

Dave Andrews

Dave Andrews (one of the Servant's Elders), his wife, Ange, and their family have spent more than thirty years living in intentional communities with marginalized people in Afghanistan, Pakistan, India, Nepal and Australia. His family now lives in Brisbane, Australia, where they established the Waiters Union, a ministry that seeks to build community with marginalized and vulnerable people. Dave is the author of numerous books, including Christi-Anarchy, Not Religion but Love, Building a Better World, *and* Compassionate Community Work.

Peter, a tall Kiwi policeman, and his wife, Adrienne, dreamed of working with Servants in Vietnam for a long time. But after taking investigatory trip with their young daughter, who was later joined by twin sisters, things didn't work out the way they had hoped they would. Instead of letting the dream disappear, however, they decided to hop 2,000 kilometers across the Tasman Sea to Sydney, Australia, rather than moving 12,000 kilometers across the Pacific Ocean to Hanoi.

Sydney, and in particular Cabramatta, contains a vast migrant population, including a large and vibrant Vietnamese community. Here all the joys and disappointments of a migrant community are found in abundance: the color and beauty of new food, dance and music; the work ethic of parents determined to give their kids what they never had; the straining gap between generations; and the drift into crime and drug abuse amongst the youth.

When they arrived in Cabramatta, Peter and Adrienne joined up with Urban Concern, a local faith-community linked to Servants. Through Urban Concern, Peter and Adrienne got to know not only the Vietnamese in Cabramatta, but also the Cambodians as well as refugees from former Yugoslavia.

Peter and his network of friends began to discuss what they might do together in the community and decided together to develop a community garden in a place that needed redemption.

They identified the Hughes Street Playground as a promising site, since it was centrally located, spacious and badly in need of rehabilitation, as it had been taken over by the 'smack squad' and had become a notorious grotto where children were not safe to play. The city authorities were delighted when they received the proposal asking for permission to lease a portion of Hughes Street Playground for this community project, and the city council not only gave them permission to use Hughes Street, but also a grant of $10,000 to fund the initial setup! Over the next twelve months, Peter and his friends met regularly with a group of local representatives, working out the details of how to proceed with the project to encourage community involvement.

They sent invitations in seven languages to an 'Open Day' to invite everybody in the wider community - especially those on the 'margins' - to join in the dream of the garden. About two hundred people turned up for the celebration, many offering suggestions about how the space could be used. The planning team also visited other community gardens around town to learn from them and also planned a training day on organic gardening. The following fall, the first eight plots were planted, then harvested, and by that winter, all twenty-three plots had been completed and allocated.

Those who have been involved in developing the garden have had to commit to work for the benefit of the whole garden, and not just their own patch. To help manage the project, a committee of three people was elected from each of the three language groups represented.

As a result of these efforts, the park has been restored. The play area that had been ceded to drug abuse has been won back for children and their families. Where there were discarded needles and garbage, now there are beautiful green gardens. All the plots are fully used and well maintained, enabling people who live in the community to gather fresh herbs and vegetables on a daily basis. Working the garden is not only productive and therapeutic for the unemployed, underemployed and elderly migrants and refugees, but it is also providing a safe place for people to forge relationships of acceptance and respect across cross-cultural divides.

The Gift of Gratitude:
Learning from the Homeless

Jason Porterfield

(USA, Canada)

For the past couple of years Jason has been a part of the Servants team based in Vancouver, Canada, ministering to the inner-city poor there. In early 2010, Jason and his wife Laura and several team mates will move to one of Indonesia's megacities to begin ministry there.

Before studying at Fuller Theological Seminary, my seminary for more than a year was the streets, and some of my greatest teachers were the homeless. Three "professors," in particular, taught me about radical gratitude in the midst of suffering.

I first met Bruce and Sheri on a roasting hot summer day in the historic district of Philadelphia. The sun was blazing, and the temperature was soaring well over 100 degrees. As I walked down the sidewalk, I saw Bruce sitting on the sidewalk, holding a cardboard sign asking for money and food. His wife, Sheri, was across the street, hoping for generosity from tourists. It was already afternoon, yet their day's accumulation had yet to be enough to buy any water, let alone food. Needless to say, they were both quite weak and dehydrated. As we ate Philly pretzels and chugged down water, our friendship began. Bruce, Sheri, and I hung out a lot that summer. As their trust in me grew, they opened up their lives to me. Bruce and Sheri were in their young thirties. Originally from York, Bruce lost his roofing job because he had made an ethical stand that had not been popular. They had recently moved to Philadelphia in hopes of finding more work. Bruce had also been diagnosed with leukemia. There were days when Bruce's radiation therapy, coupled with the intense summer heat, caused him to be so weak that Sheri and I would have to carry him to an air-conditioned restaurant to feed him.

One night in August, I was helping take a youth group around to feed and talk with the homeless. We had two meals left, and so I asked if we could visit Bruce and Sheri. When we arrived, Sheri had just finished meticulously laying out her cardboard and blanket for the night. She told me that today - unlike most days - Bruce had gotten lucky. After waiting with the other day laborers in line for a job, he had been hired to help with roofing. As we talked with Sheri, Bruce appeared in the distance, staggered toward us, then collapsed onto his bed. After roofing all day in the intense heat, the contractors had only paid him twenty dollars. In order to save money, he had walked the five miles "home" instead of taking the bus.

Faced with such suffering and injustice, I was speechless, but then Sheri broke the silence and asked us to pray for them. Before falling asleep, his skin burned bright red, Bruce prayed, "Lord, we will not worry about tomorrow. Thank you for helping Sheri and I make it through today."

Eight months later, I found myself sitting on a park bench near the beach in Santa Monica, California, opposite a strip of booming night clubs. I watched as those without homes set up their beds for the night in the park, and as across the street those who had not only one home, but multiple homes, pulled up in sports cars, Jaguars, and Rolls Royces, waiting for valets to come and attend to their needs.

As I remembered Bruce and Sheri, a rat ran by my foot, motivating me to leave the park and cross the street, the invisible wall that separated these two worlds. As I walked down a busy shopping promenade, I noticed an elderly, Irish lady who, like Bruce, was holding a sign asking for help. Typically when people ask me for help, I'm down to my last dollar and already running late to my next appointment. But on this particular night, I had time, and a friend had just given me some money with which to bless others. Feeling confident, I approached her and asked if she wanted to get a late dinner together.

"Oh no," she said gently. "I've been so thirsty, and so a few minutes ago, I closed my eyes and prayed to God for some water. When I opened my eyes, look at what was at my feet!" Lowering my eyes from her radiant smile to her feet, I was amazed to see at

191

least twenty water bottles in two grocery bags.

"Do you want to celebrate God's faithfulness with some ice cream?" I asked.

"Oh no! I can't go anywhere. I haven't finished thanking God yet."

As I walked away, deeply humbled, I thought about how quickly I move from thanking God for providing my needs today to nervously praying that He'll do the same with tomorrow's challenges. It is the poor who are helping me slowly learn the wisdom Jesus taught in Matthew 6:34: "Therefore, do not worry about tomorrow, for tomorrow will worry about its own things. Sufficient for the day is its own trouble."

The Gift of Simple Living:
Learning from our Children

Reuben and Kim

(Delhi, India)

Reuben, a lawyer, and Kim, a math and computer science honors graduate, moved from Australia into the slums of Delhi in 1995, where they continue to live, along with their two young sons, Henry and Bill.

Many of our poor Indian friends and neighbors live on about 100 rupees (about US$2.20) a day for their family. That's about 3,000 rupees (US $65) a month. By contrast, as a family, we use about 20,000 rupees (US $450) a month.

Our seven-year old son, Henry, was born here in India and often asks probing questions about God, poverty, faith and our role in it all. On hearing how much we spent every month, he was aghast and asked why we didn't live on as little as our Indian friends. After trying to justify it, by explaining that we had to spend money on many things that an Indian family wouldn't have to (such as sending a newsletter back to Australia), we acknowledged that his criticism was valid, and so, as a family, we embarked on the challenge of living on 5,000 rupees (just over US $100) for one month, choosing February because it only had 29 days.

Though we finished the month with 15 rupees (30 cents) left over, we wouldn't have made it if the month had been one day longer. Here's a rough breakdown of our expenditure for the month:

	Expense (Rupees)	US$ equivalent
Food	1,700	35
Rent	1,000	20
School fees	500	10
Transport	500	10
Giving	500	10
Miscellaneous	800	15
Total	**5,000**	**100**

We're the first to admit that experimenting like this for one month is a very far cry from experiencing it month after month for your whole life, as the poor do! We can never really know what it's like to be poor, as we always have choices that our poor friends don't. Nevertheless, we gained a little more insight into the struggles and vulnerability that the poor face every day and learned some valuable lessons.

After cutting out luxuries like cornflakes for breakfast and jam on our bread, we realized that transport by any means other that walking, cycle or bus was simply out of the question. And so we ended up doing a lot of walking! This is far from convenient or easy, especially when your kids are hot and tired and you're all feeling increasingly grumpy. In fact it can be an incredible hassle. The clean, efficient electric inner-city train system that the city had recently installed suddenly became too expensive for us, as they charge for the kids as well. The city's buses only charge for adults, but are crowded and take much longer.

We also discovered how difficult it was to be hospitable, since providing tea and biscuits (simple cookies) for guests was enough to blow the family budget for the day - and it also meant eating less that night after the guests left. I found myself becoming much stingier, as it became hard to give even a couple of rupees to beggars, and I'd find myself haggling with the mandarin seller over whether he charged 2 or 2.5 rupees per mandarin (a difference of 1 cent). And when a western friend traveled home with us and didn't offer to pay us for her ticket - something that normally wouldn't worry me - the resentment I felt ran deep. In fact, several times we had to humble ourselves to ask for repayment when normally we might have let such things go. How much more humiliating to have to beg or borrow off others in order to make ends meet.

We also found ourselves continually thinking about money and expenses, considering how we could conserve our meager resources, which made it hard to obey Jesus' exhortation "not to worry about your life, and what you will eat or drink" (Matthew 6:25).

Thankfully, we didn't have anyone fall sick during the month - and if someone had needed to go to a doctor or hospital, we would've forgotten about our experiment! But for the poor, sickness can totally consume their budget and, as a consequence, the family might not be able to pay rent. Consequently, those who are vulnerable often go to quack doctors (who may do a quick fix of symptoms but don't treat the real problem), or to moneylenders for credit.

Because our budget was tight, we tended to buy things in smaller volume that were lower in quality. For the poor, this means that they will actually spend more in the longer term while obtaining shoddier, less healthy goods. Our diet became significantly more boring through the month as interesting or quality foods were simply too expensive.

We also felt loss more acutely - such as when I dropped some food in the street and was grieved to have to throw it away. And when we hit our tennis ball over a fence during a family cricket game, we were unable to replace it. The relative cost of these losses also helped me understand the high incidence of infighting within families around us, with some small carelessness causing others to explode into a violent rage.

With fewer options of places to go and things to do, life became more tedious. (On our last day, we had to stay put at home and eat from our dwindling food supplies.) We realized why televisions are so ubiquitous in the slums; once the initial outlay is made, it's a source of cheap, brain-numbing entertainment. And little wonder that other, more dangerous temptations such as alcohol, drugs, gambling, and brothels appear attractive as ways to break out of the back-breaking monotony of poverty.

When there is only a little extra income it becomes a major decision trying to decide how it will be spent. We had to put off buying new shoes for the boys, since our budget couldn't have covered such a big purchase. And we all felt the weight of a brief phone call to Australia (100 rupees). Managing a low budget simply took us a lot more time and required more emotional energy.

Frankly it was a tough month and we were all pretty glad when it was over. We had gained a deeper insight into the frustration and sheer exhaustion of suddenly having so little control over even the smallest details of daily life. But what remained was our admiration for our neighbors who are genuinely and inescapably poor, and yet still manage to live with a sense of generosity, hospitality, celebration - and sometimes even joy - towards one another.

So all in all it was a very powerful learning experience, and we would recommend it to you to try - if your family is getting on well at the time!

If you are longing to move towards greater freedom through simple living, the following are six simple steps we can all take:

1. Inform ourselves about our true state. (John 8:32.)
Look at www.golobalrichlist.com to find out how rich we really are! Read publications from and about the poor in our own societies and in the developing world. Find out what the root causes of poverty really are – and how these can be changed.

2. Make friends among the poor, starting with one genuine friendship. (Romans 12:13 and 16.)

When we deliberately go out of our way to make friends with the poor, both in our own country and overseas, our hearts tend to be softened, we are confronted by our wealth, and we are more likely to do something about it.

3. Mix with other like minded people with whom we can be honest and mutually accountable. (Hebrews 10:24-25.)
There are other people out there who, like us, struggle with wealth. Let's seek each other out and meet together to share our burden, confess our guilt, and make plans together about what we can do.

4. Take one more step towards Christ. (Luke 12:22-34.)
Jesus knows where each of us is on our journey with Him. He doesn't expect the same step from you as He does from me or anyone else, but he does expect movement towards Him and His way of compassion. Christ calls us all to the next step on the journey of radical discipleship that demonstrates our care for God and that we care for our neighbor as we care for ourselves.

5. Hold up models of people who've done it or are doing it! (Hebrews 12:1, 13:7-8.)
Read and discuss stories of great heroes from history who've wonderfully dealt with their wealth, such as Francis of Assisi, Tohohiko Kagawa, Damien the Leper and Mother Teresa. Ask around and find others, including communities in your locality. Discuss principles you can absorb and adapt from them, and how you can work with or join them.

6. Pray for God's strength. Mark 9:23-24.
Jesus didn't promise the journey would be easy, but He did promise, in the story of the rich young man, that with God's help, it is possible to deal with our wealth (Mark 10:27).

The Gift of Life
Concluding Reflections on Simplicity

Kristin Jack

Command those who are rich in this present world not to be arrogant nor to put their hope in wealth, which is so uncertain, but to put their hope in God, who richly provides us with everything for our enjoyment. Command them to do good, to be rich in good deeds, and to be generous and willing to share. In this way they will lay up treasure for themselves as a firm foundation for the coming age, so that they may take hold of the life that is truly life.

(1 Timothy 6:17-19)

As Christians wanting to share Jesus' radical commitment to the poor, we commit ourselves to lifestyles of inner and outward simplicity, setting aside our 'right' to affluence while there are still those who live in abject poverty. We desire to be a relevant and prophetic voice in a world - and, tragically, in a Church - that is preoccupied with self, calling on those who have more than they need to share with those who have less. By so doing we will free up resources from individuals and communities dying of over-consumption and obesity in order to meet the needs of those dying of poverty. By living simple and environmentally sustainable lifestyles, we can show love for God's creation and fulfill his mandate to be caretakers of it.

But there is a flip side to this commitment. You will notice that simplicity is one of our cardinal mission principles, while celebration is one of our five community values.[16] These two go together. They hold hands in the same way that justice is knit together with mercy[17] and "righteousness and peace kiss."[18] For unless our commitment to simplicity springs out of a deep sense of gratitude, there is the danger of us falling into a cheerless legalism. In this sense, simplicity is a positive experience that overflows out of us to bless others, rather than a grim practice of self-denial. The practice of simplicity helps us to let go of all that possesses us, and gratitude helps us to acknowledge that all we have is a gift from God for the good of the whole community, for the 'commonwealth.' By holding these practices together, we root ourselves in the belief that all we have comes from the one who loves us and cares for us. Simplicity without gratitude can lead to austerity or smugness; gratitude without simplicity can lead us into the 'prosperity gospel', and a self-indulgence that forgets the poor. In both cases, we can become self-righteous or hypocritical.

When we look to Jesus, we see someone who was neither self-righteous nor hypocritical, but someone who lived with huge generosity of spirit. Someone who loved life, loved to eat and drink (yet could deny himself these things when necessary), and who loved people most of all. Jesus was able to live a life of generous overflow, because he lived in total awareness of God's care and provision for him. He lived simply, he lived freely, and he loved deeply. This surely is the way that God intends us all to live.

Earn much,
Consume little,
Hoard nothing,
Give generously,
Celebrate life. [19]
—*Viv Grigg*

Poised between two choices
Kristin Jack

here I stand
laden with your gifts
for you have given me
every good and needful thing
that I might live for you.
here I stand
the world beneath my feet
poised between two choices:
a life of privilege or of service?
a life of pleasure or of love?

here I stand
high on a mountain-top
while a slick tongue whispers
"you have worked hard,
you deserve it,
a little bit more won't hurt,
live it up,
why not?

jump, and you'll not be hurt
eat, and you'll not grow fat
take, and you'll not be tainted,
for all these lovely things
I give you now,
if you'll worship me."

Here I stand
poised between two choices
to consume your gifts like cotton-candy
with which to line my empty soul
or,
cherish life like precious manna,
bread which must be shared
among my fellow beggars
before it turns to dust.

THE SOUND OF WORLDS COLLIDING

1. Freedom of Simplicity (Harper Collins: New York, 1981), 184.
2. If you're interested, check out where you stand at www.globalrichlist.com.
3. Barrett, New Internationalist, July 1984, www.newint.org. These figures are over twenty years old now, but the picture hasn't changed; it has simply worsened. See for example Smith C, Emerson M, Passing the Plate: Why American Christians Don't Give Away More Money. Oxford University Press, 2008. This research estimates that while the overall average is 2.9% given away, most U.S. Christians give away less than 1% of their annual income.
4. Just as those of us who are honest enough to acknowledge our addictions to alcohol, drugs, or pornography need the support of recovery groups such as AA, those of us recovering from an addiction to wealth, overconsumption and the god of mammon no doubt need to be part of a supportive community as we seek freedom from bondage.
5. Luke 12:15; Colossians 3:5.
6. Mark 4:19; Matthew 19:23; 1Timothy 6:9-10.
7. Bahai is a relatively recent and eclectic religion that combines elements from all the world's major faiths, although all submit to the interpretation of Bahai's own prophet, the Baha'lluah.
8. There are many such churches throughout the Philippines, and indeed anywhere people live in desperate situations and long for a better life.
9. Hugh Todd, an artist and former newspaper cartoonist from New Zealand, lived in Manila in the 1980s.
10. This was during the people power revolution and the toppling of Marcos. Hugh, unlike many missionaries, had taken the risk of marching with his poor neighbors to protest against Marcos' corruption and suppression of human rights.
11. Along with Jenni Craig and Ian Williams, other Servants workers who had become their mentors.
12. Spread across the urban slums where Servants lived and worked were five of these Living Springs churches.
13. Lilok means 'forge' in the Tagalog language and has fraternal links with the Forge Community in Australia.
14. Onesimo is the drug rehabilitation ministry for teenagers described in "Ricco – a boy in search of his father," by Christian Schneider, found in Chapter 2 (Community).
15. They have since formed as a sending base: Philippines Servants.
16. The next chapter, "Values that Sustain Us," includes a discussion of Servants' five community values: grace, beauty, celebration, creativity and rest.
17. Micah 6:8.
18. Psalm 85:10.
19. Servants' founder.

Six

CONCLUSION

The real miracle is not that we do this work,
but that we are happy to do it.

Mother Teresa

LESSONS WE ARE LEARNING: VALUES THAT SUSTAIN US

Kristin Jack

"You ask me 'what is the most important thing?' And
I will tell you. It is People... People... People..."

Maori Proverb

The Call to Transformation

In Matthew 28:16-20 Jesus commanded us to go to all people in all nations and make disciples among them. The Greek word for disciple, 'methenes', means 'learner' or 'apprentice,' meaning that a disciple is someone who is learning to put the words of Jesus into practice. To be followers of Jesus means we have committed ourselves to a process of constant learning and relearning. It is also a process of constant letting go, and of dying to our desires for easy answers and painless solutions. In the gospels, whenever we see people queuing up to join Jesus' movement too quickly, we witness him slowing down these would-be converts, asking them to count the cost and make sure they are prepared to die to 'self' and learn to serve, rather than be served.[1] Frankly, in terms of 'mass evangelism', Jesus was a bit of a failure. He really did seem more concerned with quality of discipleship than with quantity of numbers.

Jesus made it tough to become a follower. When he sent out his disciples, he stripped them of their material possessions: "Take nothing for the journey except a staff—no bread, no bag, no money in your belts. Wear sandals but not an extra tunic."[2] He also taught his followers that their treatment of the poor was synonymous with their treatment of him: "Whatever you did not do for one of the least of these brothers of mine, you did not do for me."[3] In that same passage, he connects our salvation with our response to the destitute and the suffering. The apostle John elaborates on this by saying "whoever has the world's goods and sees his brother in need, and closes his heart against him - how does the love of God abide in him?"[4] Jesus entered the world homeless and became a refugee (to Egypt) before his first birthday. He walked and taught among the people as a poor man, with 'nowhere to lay his head.'

Compassion for and identification with the poor and marginalized are a huge part of Jesus' character - and so it should also be a defining quality of his followers.[5]

The way of Jesus was to call his disciples to be with him as he went about Judea ministering to the poor, the sick, the disturbed, the distressed, and the possessed. Afterwards, as a group, they would slip away to quiet places to reflect on all they had experienced – both their successes and failures – and to suck out every ounce of learning that they could from the life Jesus was showing them.[6] When Jesus sent out the disciples he gave them the following instructions, "As you go, preach this message: 'The Kingdom of heaven is near. Heal the sick, raise the dead, cleanse those who have leprosy, drive out demons. Freely you have received, freely give.'"[7] The disciples learned by being plunged into the real world

CONCLUSION

of poverty, suffering and opposition (both political and demonic) - into a life of ministry interspersed with reflection and prayer. As Viv Grigg has written elsewhere: "discipleship has to be taught in the context of a Jesus-style ministry to the poor - in the context of rejecting pride and status seeking, power and economic security."[8]

Those who minister among people living in the midst of suffering, seeking to live out the love of Jesus, will always be confronted with the pain and messy dilemmas of life. But despite all its difficulties (indeed, probably because of them), living this way is transformative - first and foremost for those who come hoping to be agents of transformation. As Mick Duncan has said elsewhere, the highest task of the Kingdom worker is "to seek Jesus through many tears, to be a sojourner not a settler, to have the courage to become someone we have never been before." After more than twenty-five years of living among the urban poor, praying and working to see their communities transformed by the power of Christ, we have learned some hard lessons about how to sustain this over the long haul. The most crucial of these is that God is much more interested in who we are becoming as people, than he is in our 'results' or lists of achievements. Doing flows out of being, and not the other way around. And our being is first and foremost grounded in God's extravagant, unconditional love for each of us.

For those of us born into success and image obsessed cultures, this is not easy to grasp. It requires that we set our ambitions on simply being a disciple and companion of Jesus, rather than being driven by any deeper need or loftier agenda. Put another way, our personal goal is to become more like Jesus, and our vision is to see his Kingdom coming in whatever place he sends us. But whether or not we are 'successful', well, we have to leave that up to God. As Mother Teresa said, *"God has not called me to be successful, He has called me to be faithful"*.

A second key strategy is to look for 'people of peace.' When we come into a situation of brokenness, pain and need, wanting to see deep and abiding change for the better, the first thing we should do is wait on God and prayerfully seek out a "worthy person" - the person of peace - before launching into mission.[9] God has always

203

gone before us, and there are always signs of his Kingdom there already, but we must ask God for the 'eyes to see.' The "worthy" to whom Jesus is referring here are those who are moved by the things that move God (sickness, hunger, suffering, death, violence, injustice, abuse, addictions etc), who love those around them, and who are prepared to get their hands dirty and do something about it. People of compassion and action. People who are already trying to help those in need. You have read about many such people in this book already. As we gather with those people, praying that God's Kingdom[10] will flow through us into this place, good plans from the heart of God and earthed in the local situation will emerge. Filipino theologian and activist Melba Maggay urges us to 'nurture a strategic minority':

> Students of social change tell us that it is better to aim at consensus within a strategic minority rather than to waste time and breath at soliciting the conformity of the majority. Since a movement for change involves vision and sacrifice it is not possible to start with the many. Very few people can see ten steps ahead of them. Most are too enclosed in the realities of the present to be able to imagine an alternative future. It takes a lot of imagination to believe that with the coming of Christ, a new order has come into being.[11]

As people pray, dream, and share about their experiences, the resources needed to carry out the vision will emerge—initially from the group itself, then the surrounding community, and beyond. If we wait on God and trust our plans to him, he will provide what is needed, no matter how much that may be.[12]

Yet if we are needs or agenda driven, it is so easy for us to rush in and begin our work the other way around. For those of us who hail from the corporate, results driven cultures of the West (and more affluent parts of Asia), it is so tempting for us to start by bringing in the kind of money that will ensure our wonderful strategies have an impact. Then secondly, taking the corporate approach, we use our impressive financial resources to attract and recruit 'highly qualified staff', then train them up on how to implement 'our strategic plan'. But the way Jesus shows us in the gospels tips this approach up-side down. First, we are told to

CONCLUSION

find good people; then we come up with a good plan together; and finally, whatever resources are needed will follow by faith. God will always give 'enough' to willing people with good plans, in order to do what must be done. He always does.

For missional communities that live among the poor, local churches and grass roots development workers, this is a natural way of working. Those who live at the local neighborhood level are in a great position to 'seek out those worthy people' or the 'people of peace' that Jesus was talking about, those gems whom bigger, better resourced groups probably won't ever notice. In fact, all of us will struggle to notice them at first - they will most likely be poor, uneducated and needy themselves[13] - but we must ask God for the eyes to see them, and for the providential circumstances in which to meet. It takes time and patience to develop these kind of eyes, eyes that can look beyond broken, rough exteriors and see the treasure buried inside.

God has put each of us on this earth for a purpose and a vocation: "for we are God's work of art, created in Christ Jesus to do good works,"[14] or as Rabbi Abraham Herschel has put it, *"the meaning of life is to build our life as if it were a work of art."* To be living a life of discipleship is to be involved in building masterpieces: works of love and beauty. We allow the Holy Spirit to do His creative, healing work in us, and we invest our life in others, helping them to discover that they too are God's work of art, a being of incredible beauty, with enormous power that they can choose to use creatively or selfishly. To be someone who makes disciples is to see the gifts and potential in others, the work of art buried in the crude rock, the masterpiece waiting to emerge. We need to ask God to give us the eyes of an artist as we nurture those around us.

Those of us who lead others, make disciples, plant churches or facilitate development need to think of ourselves as loving gardeners working over the long haul - ten years or longer if we dream of being those who reproduce themselves thirty-fold, sixty-fold, or even a hundred-fold.[15] What the poor need are not cosmetic changes but transformation that will sink deep roots into their structures and relationships, catalyzed by local agents of

205

change who bear the kind of fruit that reproduces over and over again.[16] But this patient, incarnational approach requires us to be prayerful and attentive in all that we do, watching to see where God's Spirit is already at work in our communities and in the lives of those around us, waiting to see his Kingdom break in among us, listening for the voice of his Spirit to beckon us to join in. He calls us all to be good gardeners. He calls us all to be waiters. He calls us to be lovers. He calls us to be servants.

But how do we 'seek Jesus through many tears' and 'have the courage to become someone we have never been before' without being destroyed in the process? How do we sustain this commitment over the long-haul? How do we hang in there for the length of time needed in order to see long-term transformation of people's lives and communities? In the early years of Servants, we had many cases of workers crashing and burning as they pushed themselves too hard and too low in pursuit of the gospel ideals that had captivated them. Over time we came to realise that with our five principles of *servanthood, simplicity, incarnation, wholism* and *community,* we still had not embraced the fullness of what Jesus was calling us to do and to be. As we reflected on this, five more community values of *grace, beauty, celebration, creativity* and *rest* began to emerge. These are not set up in opposition to the original five principles, but to fill them out and bring balance to them - and to our lives. They capture more of the fullness and richness of the gospel vision. They help us to live more sustainably and more centered on Christ.

Grace

"There is no deep knowing of God without a deep knowing of self, and no deep knowing of self without a deep knowing of God."
John Calvin[17]

Who we are and all that we do is rooted in and sustained by God's lavish, unearned love, favor and forgiveness towards us. This profound grace delivers us from unhealthy striving, competition and condemnation of ourselves or judgment of others. It is only by abiding in the presence of Christ - the only source of this loving grace - that we can be equipped for lives of worship, service, justice and compassion.

Apart from him, we can do nothing.[18]

All our striving means nothing if it is not an overflow of grace and love. Paul understood this in a profound way: *"if I have the faith that can move mountains, but have not love, I am nothing. If I give all I possess to the poor, and even allow my body to be destroyed, but have not love, it means nothing."*[19] Our goal must be genuine love lived out in grace, and not a striving to live lower or better or more sacrificially than anyone else. Genuine love is more important than teeth-gritted sacrifice. Transformative relationships are built out of love, not 'duty'.

The greatest lessons we have learned are about grace. We can only survive if we live by grace. God's grace towards us, grace towards one another, and grace towards ourselves. We have come to that point where we realize that the Christian life is not so much about us striving to be like Jesus (though, of course, we long for that), but about us allowing Jesus to live his life of love in and through us. We have to learn to stop struggling to be 'super-spiritual' or 'super-Christian', and instead simply let ourselves become more real. For we are beginning to understand that the path of following Jesus is about us becoming more human and more vulnerable.

Paul came to realize this lesson of grace in his own ministry, and he wrote: *"And I am the least of the apostles...but, by the grace of God I am what I am, and his grace towards me was not without effect. No, I worked harder than all of them - yet not I but the grace of God that was within me."*[20] Later, he wrote: *"He told me: 'my grace is sufficient for you, for my power is made perfect in your weakness; therefore I can delight in weakness...and in difficulties; for when I am weak, I am strong."*[21] Paul had come to the point where he could honestly face himself and all his weaknesses, without needing to hide them or pretend he was something he was not. We have begun to realize that genuine self-awareness is essential. If we are not aware of our own gifts and shadows, of how we react under stress or in the midst of conflict, our hidden motivations and unconscious responses will blindside us when we least expect it. To help us along in this journey towards this 'grace-full' self-awareness, we have found both Myers-Briggs[22] and the Enneagram[23] to be invaluable tools. We also highly recommend David Benner's beautiful book, *The Gift of Being Yourself*,[24] which is a goldmine of helpful insights.

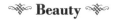

Beauty

"Beauty is to the spirit what food is to the flesh. It fills an emptiness in you which nothing else can fill." Frederick Buechner

Because God is the author of all beauty - in our lives, homes, communities and world—we honor God and renew our souls by recognizing and creating beauty. In particular, we want to see and celebrate the beauty inherent in ourselves, our teammates, our neighbors, and of course, in God. We easily notice the beauty in a sunset, a work of art, or even in the vitality of a healthy young woman or man,[25] though over time we can grow jaded even with these signposts of our creator. But we must ask God to give us the eyes to see his beauty buried everywhere, even in pain and poverty, even among those crippled with disease and approaching death. Francis of Assisi traced his 'real conversion' from that time he climbed down from his muscular horse and embraced a wandering leper, giving him the kiss of peace as he did so. Earlier Francis, raised to love beauty and the finer things in life, had always held a deep fear and revulsion for those suffering from this dreaded disease. But after allowing himself to see and embrace God's beauty in the leper, he was freed to see it everywhere. A deep and disturbing truth lies here. If we surround ourselves with 'beautiful things' – when beauty is defined by the most superficial voices of our culture (the 'beauty myth'): shining models, glossy magazines, shimmering T.V's – when we surround ourselves with these things, we become less and less able to embrace and love the weak, the broken, the not-pretty – either in others or in ourselves. We become less able to follow the Biblical injunction to "not be proud, but to hang-out with those of low status" (Romans 12:16). Jesus also possessed this ability to see God's beauty everywhere - in the sparrow, the wild flowers, the heads of grain, the reddened skies, the poor and the sick, the widow's act of giving, the tears of a fallen woman,[26] and in reckless acts of love and care:

> *While he was in Bethany, reclining at the table in the home of a man known as Simon the Leper, a woman came with an alabaster jar of very expensive perfume, made of pure nard. She broke the jar and poured the perfume on his head. Some of those present were saying indignantly to one another, "Why this waste of perfume? It could have been sold for more than a year's wages and the money given to the poor." And they rebuked her harshly. "Leave her alone," said Jesus. "Why are you bothering her? She has done a beautiful thing to me. The poor you will always have with you, and you can help them any time you want. But you will not always have me. She did what she could. She poured perfume on my body beforehand to prepare for my burial. I tell you the truth, wherever the gospel is preached throughout the world, what she has done will also be told, in memory of her."[27]*

We are coming to see the deep and mysterious connection that exists between beauty and suffering, and how - in this present order of things - we cannot have one without the other. But we worship a God who is always seeking to transform suffering into beauty,[28] for this is the way of Jesus and his Kingdom.

Our commitment to simplicity and our frequent exposure to suffering and injustice can make us forget this, and what an incredibly beautiful universe God has already created - and for no other purpose but that we and God should enjoy it together![29] The fact is that God designed us to enjoy all that he created, to rejoice in it and to give him glory for it.[30] In particular, God calls us to see and celebrate the beauty inherent in ourselves and in each other. Therefore, in our lives, homes, communities and world – no matter how small or simple they be - we seek to honor God and renew our souls by seeing and creating beauty. We will plant flowers, use color, drape fabrics, hang pictures, play music—and give God thanks for all of it!

 **Celebration**

"Go and enjoy choice food and sweet drinks, and give some to those who have nothing. This day is sacred to our Lord... the joy of the Lord is your strength." Nehemiah 8:10

God calls us to be a grateful people and a generous people - generous with our love, generous with our time, generous with our praise, generous with our money. The Old Testament is full of lavish festivals[31] where the people of God pooled their money (their tithes and offerings) in order to celebrate God's presence and goodness, and to bless the poor.

In mission among the poor it is so easy for us to be dragged down by a sense of failure, despairing that our little efforts aren't making any difference at all. And so quickly these thoughts will become self-fulfilling prophesies for us. Instead, we have learned to consciously mark every milestone and achievement - no matter how small - with some kind of celebration. Aligned with this, we want to become people with generous souls, refusing to take ourselves (though not our cause) too seriously. It is so much healthier to be able to laugh at our own follies and foibles (instead of despairing over them) and to undermine our pomp and pride with playfulness and humor.[32] Jesus said that it would be those who become like children who would enter his Kingdom,[33] and children like nothing better than to play and celebrate. To this end, we will use song, poetry, drama, dance, food, stillness, silence, and even our tears as a form of worship to celebrate God's goodness and presence among us.

Every Tuesday our team here in Cambodia gathers for a shared meal. It's an open table, a blessed opportunity to invite friends and strangers to join us. There is little else in life as 'spiritual' as eating together, which is why it features so prominently in the Scriptures. After the shared meal we worship, share our struggles and joys with one another, and pray together. This is often a time when tears flow as we try to help 'carry one another's burdens'.[34] Each Servants team establishes its own different rhythms of prayer, table fellowship, worship and sharing, but whatever the variations, we have learnt that these are sacred and essential if we are to sustain each other over the long haul. *"Finally my brothers, rejoice in the Lord! It is no trouble for me to write the same things to you again, and it is a safe guard for you...Rejoice in the Lord always. I will say it again: Rejoice!"*[35]

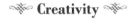

Creativity

"The Christian is the one whose imagination should fly beyond the stars." Francis Schaeffer

Just as God made us to enjoy beauty, he made us to be creative - for by creating, we show forth the presence of God in our lives. Even holding together the challenges of living simply *and* living a life of celebration forces us to look to God for his creativity!

By allowing our senses, imaginations, minds and bodies to fulfill their God-given potentials for creativity, we glorify God. It pleases God and does our souls good when we create. Team-mates are always encouraged to give their 'right-brains' some freedom and to try writing or telling stories or poems; to try painting, making music, cooking, sewing, weaving, or any expression of themselves through art. From the Scriptures we learn that the Holy Spirit not only empowers us with gifts of healing and power, but also with gifts of art and craft.[36]

By embracing the value of creativity, we seek to release the creative power inherent both in ourselves and in the lives of the poor. For this author, creative writing and reading are tremendously therapeutic, and far from seeing them as 'time wasters' that distract me from time with my neighbors, they have become sources of renewal and reflection, something that help me discern what God is doing in my life and in the life of those around me. They help renew me, so that I can carry on.

 Rest

> *"Therefore, since the promise of entering his rest still stands, let us be careful that none of us be found to have fallen short of it...There remains, then, a Sabbath-rest for the people of God; for anyone who enters God's rest also rests from his own work, just as God did from his. Let us, therefore, make every effort to enter that rest, so that no one will fall by following examples of disobedience."*
>
> Hebrews 4:1 and 9-11

From the Scriptures we learn that the life God calls us to is replete with cycles of work and rest - weekly Sabbaths, frequent celebrations and regular holy-days (holidays). God commands us to rest in order to be refreshed, be still, enjoy his creation, and deepen our relationship with him and one another. The Sabbath was *given* to us for our *rest* and worship, designed to *bless* humanity, and not the other way round.[37] We are commanded to regularly draw away from our work and to rest in God.[38] Times of quietness, solitude and reflection are all necessary for our bodies and souls to remain healthy. Therefore, we need to be committed to regular rhythms of work, rest and reflection, keeping true Sabbaths, frequent celebrations, regular holidays and Sabbaticals, in order to stay close to God and our loved ones. Finding space for exercise is also important. Jesus (and Paul) did a heck of a lot of long-distance walking in the course of their ministries!

In the midst of crowded, noisy, often-polluted urban slums, all of this is difficult. But for survival and longevity, we need to periodically retreat to places of stillness and quiet where we can be alone with God and our own soul (and catch up on our sleep!). Frequently in the Gospels we find mention of Jesus retiring to a hillside in order to spend down-time with his Father. If we want to operate in the flow of God's Spirit as Jesus did, we also must seek out these lonely places with God. *"Come to me, all you who are weary and burdened, and I will give you rest. Take my yoke upon you and learn from me, for I am gentle and humble in heart, and you will find rest for your souls. For my yoke is easy and my burden is light."*[39] For Susan and I, all of these lessons were learned through hard, personal experience. At the end of our first five years in Cambodia, we were broken people, and nearly burned out. We had seen too many friends die. We had watched too many hopes and dreams crumble. We had wrestled with too many intractable issues that never seemed to improve. Within three months of our arrival in Cambodia, we had been made leaders of a large team, and each team member was struggling with stress and dilemmas - and frankly, we didn't have the skills or maturity to pull that off. Untreated stress easily mutates into conflict, and indeed our team life had gradually become full of conflict and criticism. Instead of building each other up, we had begun to tear each other down. Towards the end of that period, Susan and I returned to New Zealand for three months home leave, and on the way, we participated in an International Servants gathering in Manila. I hadn't realised just how low I was until a worship time on the last morning of the large gathering. During the last song I broke down and began to weep uncontrollably for the next three quarters of an hour. A deep sense of failure and waves of despair kept sweeping over me. For a fairly unemotional person who seldom cries, this was shocking, and I realised just how broken I was. Susan and I knew that the writing was on the wall, and that we simply could not survive this way.

Desperate not to become 'burn-out statistics' who leave the field prematurely, we returned to New Zealand and took on spiritual directors,[40] and spent much of our leave time discussing with each other and others how we could live more sustainably back in Cambodia: physically, emotionally, spiritually and communally. We were also able to invite some team building coaches to come and spend time with us as a team, so that we could learn better ways of supporting each other. Amazingly, miraculously, God turned it all around. Within a few months, both Susan and I were back leading the team with a renewed sense of hope and vision. Within a couple of years, our community had become one of the most loving, nurturing, well-performing teams we have ever been a part of.

Over the past twenty-seven years, Servants has learned painfully about the cost of doing mission amongst the urban poor, and how crucial it is to build strong teams, provide sensitive pastoral care and encourage each team member to know their boundaries and develop a clear self-care plan. We have moved from a single 'International Coordinator' trying to oversee multiple fields, to a team leadership structure, supported by an Eldership made up of seasoned women and men who act as our 'wisdom bank.' Instead of throwing people into the deep-end to see whether they will sink or swim, a worker's first year on the field is now devoted to their 'formation.' As well as language and culture learning, new workers are mentored through a series of readings and reflections by more experienced team-mates.

We have learned to see every individual life as truly precious (including our own!), and to rejoice over every seed sown and every person touched. And this really is what this book is all about. It is a celebration of the many lives whose stories you have just read. Many of them were poor people whose lives might have easily seemed small and insignificant. But no life and no person is insignificant - each one is of inestimable worth - for we worship a God who *"raises up the poor from the dust and lifts up the needy from the ash heap and seats them with princes, yes even with the princes of the people."*[41]

Our vision in Servants is to see communities of hope, compassion and justice spring up in every city of the world, on every continent, starting in Asia, spreading back to the West, and then on and on... communities of those who genuinely want to learn how to love God, how to love neighbor, and how to follow Jesus together. Communities of those who genuinely want to make a difference - no matter how small - in the face of the poverty, oppression and violence that will otherwise sweep away all before them. We want to take up Brian McLaren's[42] call to be those who

CONCLUSION

plant "un-terror cells" all around the world, cells of creative non-violence and caring community development that will send out the message that, yes, Jesus is risen, and his teachings and Lordship are changing everything. Will you join us? Will you put your hand to the plow along side us and the other missional communities springing up all over the world? Do you want to be known as one of those 'who have come to turn the world up-side down,' as the first followers of Jesus were known?[43] Now is the time to hear the call that the prophet Isaiah heard, and to give the answer Isaiah gave:

With the burning coal he touched my lips and said,
"Your guilt is taken away, all your sins are atoned for."
Then I heard the voice of the Lord asking,
"Whom shall I send? And who will go for us?"
And so I said, "Here I am, send me…"
Isaiah 6:7-8

1. e.g., Luke 9:57-62, 14:25-34, 17:7-10, 18:22; John 6:41-66.
2. Mark 6:8-9.
3. Matthew 25:45.
4. 1 John 3:17; see also Luke 6:24-26; 16:19-31, 19:8-9.
5. e.g., Philippians 2:5-11 and Matthew 9:36. Of course, Jesus also loved the rich he encountered (e.g. Mark 10:21) and was more than willing to spend time with them too – there is no record in the gospels of Jesus ever turning down one of their dinner invitations! Yet his encounters with the rich and powerful always challenged them to release their grip on wealth and power, and to turn to embrace the poor, the marginalized and those suffering from injustice (e.g. Mark 10:17-25; Luke 19:2-10; Luke 7:36-50; Luke 12:13:21; Luke 14:1-14; Luke 16:19-31).
6. e.g., Mark 6:7-13, 30-31; 9:23-31.
7. Matthew 10:6-8.
8. Viv Grigg, Companion to the Poor, 21-22.
9. See Matthew 10:11 and Luke 10:6.
10. Matthew 10:8.
11. Melba Maggay, Survival Strategies, 7.
12. This is the lesson of the fish and the loaves in Luke 9:10-17.
13. 1 Corinthians 1:26-28.
14. Ephesians 2:10.
15. See John 15:1-9 and Mark 4:20.
16. Check out the "oaks of righteousness" mentioned in Isaiah 61:1-4, and where they have come from, and what they can do for their community once established.

17. John Calvin, Institutes of the Christian Religion, 1536 edition, cited in David Benner, The Gift of Being Yourself (InterVarsity Press: 2004), 20.
18. John 15:5.
19. 1 Corinthians 13:2-3.
20. 1 Corinthians 15:9-10.
21. 2 Corinthians 12:9-10.
22. Go to www.myersbriggs.org to learn more.
23. See www.enneagraminstitute.com or Richard Rohr's The Enneagram: A Christian Perspective (Crossroad Publishing: 2006) for an introduction to this system of personality typology.
24. David Benner, The Gift of Being Yourself (InterVarsity Press: 2004).
25. And of course the great danger here is of being seduced by that form of beauty which runs only skin deep, of being seduced by the so-called 'beauty myth.' It is this seduction that advertising, fashion and pornography industries thrive on. Perhaps this is the battle for the heart that Dostevsky was referring to when he wrote, "Beauty is not only a majestic thing, it is also a mysterious thing. There God and the Devil strive for mastery, and the battleground is the heart of man."
26. Matthew 6:26-29; 16:2-3; 9:35-36; Luke 21:1-4; Luke 7:36-50.
27. Mark 14:3-9.
28. Isaiah 61:1-3
29. Think about your tongue for a minute: God made it covered with thousands and thousands of nerve ends just so we could savour every nuance of taste. And he made our eyes so they can revel in a myriad of colours and shades, our skin to embrace and differentiate all kinds of textures, touches and caresses. All of this was extravagant and unnecessary on God's part.
30. Psalm 104, especially verse 15.
31. Deuteronomy 12:1-25; 14:22-29.
32. Proverbs 17:22. As well as learning to laugh, we must learn to weep; as well as learning to celebrate, we must also learn how to lament (Ecclesiastes 3:4). In my experience, the poor in most developing nations are far better at both these things than Westerners, and it is from them that we must learn. The word joy appears 242 times in Scripture; 'rejoice' appears 156 times; 'celebrate' appears 67 times; thanksgiving appears 100 times. Obviously, the Scriptures have something to say about what is life-giving that many of us more sophisticated folk have missed.
33. Mark 10:15.
34. Galatians 6:2.
35. Philippians 3:1 and 4:4.
36. In Exodus 31:1-5, the Lord tells Moses, "See, I have chosen Bezalel son of Uri, the son of Hur, of the tribe of Judah, and I have filled him with the Spirit of God, with skill, ability and knowledge in all kinds of crafts—to make artistic designs for work in gold, silver and bronze, to cut and set stones, to work in wood, and to engage in all kinds of craftsmanship."
37. Mark 2:27.
38. Hebrews 4:9-11.
39. Matthew 11:28-30.
40. In many countries it is now possible to engage with a 'spiritual director,' someone who has been trained to listen and pray attentately and help you make sense of where God is present in your circumstances (both good and bad). Every Servants worker is now expected to engage with a spiritual director or equivalent.
41. Psalm 113:7-8.
42. Brian McLaren, Everything Must Change (Thomas Nelson: 2007), p129-130. An outstanding book.
43. Acts 17:6 KJV.

AFTERWORD

Dave Andrews

(Servants Elder)

A nd what shall I say of these men and women? Shall I pity them? I have cried with them as I have heard their stories of heartache and heartbreak. But I cannot say we should pity them. For though they have sown their lives in tears, they have harvested the fruit of the Spirit with smiles. Shall I praise them for their extraordinary commitment to simplicity, solidarity and service? No. It would only embarrass them. They don't want awards. They want fellow travelers to accompany them on their journey into a deeper kind of community with the world's poor, deeper than most of us had hitherto thought was possible. So what shall I say without pity or praise?

All I can say is that I love them. I love their joyous passion for Jesus and their courageous compassion for their neighbors. I love their willingness to take risks in order to flesh out the love of God in the harsh places of our world where hurting people feel most God-forsaken. I love their capacity to be hard-core on the one hand and soft-hearted on the other - both at the same time. I love the fact that they can stay on track in terms of their mission, and yet still stop every now and then to help others of us who are struggling to keep up. And I love their ability to take the issues seriously, but not themselves - bringing a delightful, whacky sense of humor to the awfully serious business of service.

It is my hope that as you reflect on these stories, you will come to love these men and women too. And who knows: we may even find ourselves not only admiring them, but imitating them as well.

EPILOGUE

POEMS OF GRACE, BEAUTY AND CALLING

Kristin Jack

Wounded Healer

You know me and you love me
even in the darkness of my fear,
you are close and you are calling
even in my wretched gut-despair,
you know me and you love me
and you ache to make me whole,
you take my million broken pieces
and mould them into one,
you weave my light against my shadow
braiding lines of beauty, threads of grace,
till each scar is like stigmata
a jagged lightening trace,
revealing all that's hidden
all I could not face,
for you use my shards of weeping
as you build your masterpiece,
drawing real self out of darkness
to stand in sacred space,
each piece of love
and pain and failure
held by holy scars
till I be-come
like you:
a wounded healer
with broken hands;
the breath of God
in flesh of man.

On Seeing Royalty in the Street

Bobbing through the indifferent traffic
and the belched-up fumes
of the out-wardly mobile
a small nugget of joy laughs
in the face of all that is so vulnerable.

Those two eyes which must have seen
the lack of all things but poverty
shine like coals
dark embers lit from within.
Across one shoulder
a rice-sack of scrap
trails like a sash or a robe
its train filled
with tin-cans like diamonds
and a million other dreams besides.

She carries her weight
with the grace of the high-born
and those dark bare feet
should fill sequin and silver
the way they glide
across tar-seal and dust
proving once more
that even in a world that crushes and binds
trading innocence for cash
children are made for a Kingdom.

A Poem for Myself, the Social Worker

You said you loved me,
but you were too scared to touch me,
your fear wouldn't let your arms unfold
and embrace my weakness.
You said you loved me,
but when you talked to me,
you talked of the weather and of money,
of foolish things that fade.

You would not look me in the eyes
for the things that I was hiding;
you were afraid that you would see it,
that I'd tell you,
and that it would become part of you also:
another burden to carry,
another nail in your cross.
You said you loved me,
but your eyes wandered,
as you wondered how to leave politely.

You asked me to speak,
but did not listen,
especially to what I could not tell you,
for your ears were straining much further
than my voice could carry:
you were listening for a dying voice within.

You said you loved me,
but your hands gripped your heart
in a vice of uncertainty that betrayed your words.
You would not give me your heart;
You were afraid,
afraid it really was all you owned.

Ask me where I was.

And still I hear it
on and on
in the hidden corners of my mind
that eternal scream
which echoes
down the corridors of time,
refusing to be silenced
it accuses me
of passivity, thus
an accessory to crime.

And still I see it
that spreading stain
a wound that never heals
that bloodied mud
that asks me where I was
that asks me what I saw:
all the children dying
in the hidden corners
of a distant foreign famine,
in a small forgotten war.

So I pray my prayers
I pay my tithe
I read my Bible every day,
I live in plenty
I sleep in peace,
and offer praises to Our God:
that though you are there,
I am here,
and so your pain is far away,
a different world
I pray to never know;

for I hope to live a blessed life
where my hands are clean,
my heart stays pure,
and there'll be no stains on me.

And yet, and yet,
there are those awful moments
unguarded and unbidden
when your screams finally reach my ears
and you ask me if my Jesus
really is that same Jesus
who was tortured for his faith
crucified for his love,
and there are those awful moments
I finally see the terror in your eyes,
and you make me wonder
if He will one day ask me
where I was and what I saw
when His children were all dying
in a distant foreign corner
in a small forgotten war.

APPENDIX A

For more information about Servants to Asia's Urban Poor, go to www.servantsasia.org

To obtain further copies of this book, please contact your nearest Servants Office:

Canada:
PO Box # 88195, Chinatown, Vancouver, B.C. V6A 4A5, Canada.
E-mail admin.canada@servantsasia.org

United Kingdom:
30 Osborne Road, Earlsdon, Coventry CV5 6DY, United Kingdom.
E-mail uk@servantsasia.org
To contact the Servants Southall/London team:
E-mail southall@servantsasia.org

United States:
4092 Carlisle Pike PMB 292, Mechanicsburg, PA 17050, USA.
E-mail usa@servantsasia.org

Switzerland:
Hegenheimerstrasse 193, CH-4055, Basel, Switzerland.
E-mail swissinfo@servantsasia.org

Australia:
PO Box 259, Red Hill, QLD 4059, Australia.
E-mail australia@servantsasia.org

New Zealand:
PO Box 19-404, Avondale, Auckland 1746, New Zealand.
E-mail nz@servantsasia.org

Cambodia:
PO Box 538, Phnom Penh, Cambodia.
E-mail cambodia@servantsasia.org

Philippines:
PO Box AC 569, Quezon City 1109, Philippines.
E-mail philippines@servantsasia.org

Servants teams also work in two other Asian countries. However, for security reasons, please contact these through our International Administrator at uk@servantsasia.org

Servants also has 'western teams' in the cities of London (Southall, a largely Asian suburb) and Vancouver (working amongst street people and drug users).

THE SOUND OF WORLDS COLLIDING

LIKE-MINDED GROUPS:

There are several other incarnational missions that Servants has close working relationships with, brother and sister movements that we are more than happy to recommend. Below is a list of some our key partner groups. We encourage you to check out their websites for more information on short and long term opportunities for deeper involvement.

A Rocha - Servants also partners with A Rocha, a Christian organization committed to valuing creation and promoting research and preservation of the natural environment. The name 'A Rocha' comes from the Portuguese for "the Rock," as their first initiative was in Portugal. A Rocha projects are frequently cross-cultural, share a community emphasis, and focus on scientific research, practical conservation and environmental education. Servant's workers offset air travel (carbon emissions) by investing equivalent amounts in A Rocha projects.

www.arocha.org

InnerCHANGE - based out of the U.S. InnerCHANGE is a Christian order composed of missionaries ministering and living incarnationally among the poor and striving to follow the Lord God's injunction to "act justly and to love mercy and to walk humbly with your God". InnerCHANGE teams currently work in several cities in the U.S, in Venezuela, Romania and Cambodia.

www.innerchange.org

Servant Partners - based out of the U.S, Servant Partners is a wholistic church planting movement working in Bangkok, Mexico City, Manila, and other locations in the Middle East and North Africa. Servants Partners offers internships in L.A and the Philippines that help young people discern their calling to the poor.

www.servantpartners.org

Urban Expression - is an urban mission agency that recruits, equips, deploys and networks teams pioneering creative and relevant expressions of the Christian church in inner city areas. Urban Expression has since 1997 deployed a number of church planting teams in East London, Manchester and Glasgow, from which new churches are gradually developing. In 2004, in response to several requests, Urban Expression Associates was formed as a network of church planters and others involved in urban mission who share our core values and want to participate in a learning community.

www.urbanexpression.org.uk

Urban Neighbourhoods of Hope - UNOH's vision is to raise-up follows of Jesus who can help release neighbourhoods from urban poverty in Asian-Pacific cities. In the early '90's Ash and Anji Barker began UNOH as a missional order working among the poor in a multicultural suburb of Melbourne, Australia. Other UNOH communities have been spread to six more needy neighbourhoods in Melbourne, to Sydney - and to the massive Klong Toey slum of Bangkok, Thailand.

www.unoh.org

Urban Vision - Based in the city of Wellington, New Zealand, U.V describes itself as "a contemporary Order following Jesus on the margins". They organise themselves as a group of households and ministries who focus on building life-giving relationships with those so often marginalized from the mainstream of society, and are committed to doing justice in the midst of urban poverty. Some U.V workers have gained experience in incarnational ministry with U.V before relocating to developing world cities with Servants; while at least one long term Servants family has relocated from a developing world context and discovered a sense of continuity by joining U.V upon their return. We are all greatly encouraged by this two way flow!

www.urbanvision.org.nz

Waiters Union - The Waiters Union is a network of residents in one of Brisbane's (Australia) poorer, more multi-cultural suburbs. Waiters Union seeks to follow in the radical tradition of Jesus, and are committed to developing a sense of community in this locality with neighbours, especially those who are marginalised. Over the years, many Servants workers have served apprenticeships with the

Waiters Union as part of their training for incarnational ministry.

www.waitersunion.org

Dave and Ange Andrews, the founders of the Waiters Union, have also launched 'Plan B' – a prophetic call for Christians to return to the teachings Jesus gave us in the Beatitudes.

www.wecan.be

Word Made Flesh - Word Made Flesh is called and committed to serve Jesus among the most vulnerable of the world's poor. Beginning in 1994, Chris Heuertz, his wife Phileena, and half a dozen friends sought to serve Christ, one another and the poor in Chennai, India. Today it has staff and short term workers serving in more than 12 cities in 11 countries all around the world.

www.wordmadeflesh.com

MORE ENDORSEMENTS FOR THE
SOUND OF WORLDS COLLIDING

"The pages of this book are coated with dust from the slums from which these stories emanate. As you open its cover, prepare for the onslaught of smells, sounds and flavours of India, Cambodia, the Philippines and other places. You won't find abstract missiology here, but theology that emerges from rich, real stories, written about real people by real incarnational servants."

MIKE FROST Author of 'Exiles', co author of 'The Shaping of Things to Come', and Vice Principal of Morling Theological College, Sydney

"Servants is the one organisation in all the reporting I have done that challenges me to the core. My original impressions were right : incarnational faith living like this is a call to run not just a race but a marathon. My prayer is that many more will put on their running shoes and join them."

ROB HARLEY Broadcaster and Filmmaker, NZ

"This book is a challenge to all of us who care about poverty, to see what a radical Jesus-centred approach really looks like. It is full of human stories that move the heart and point towards the transforming love of Jesus. The principles and values by which the Servants teams are seeking to live are inspiring. Even more inspiring is to see how they translate into an incarnational ministry in urban slums overflowing with the love and presence of Christ. I warmly recommend this book."

PETER GRANT International Director, Tearfund UK